EVERYDAY LIFE IN ANCIENT
EGYPT
& MESOPOTAMIA

LORNA OAKES
PHILIP STEELE

southwater

This edition is published by Southwater

Southwater is an imprint of Anness Publishing Ltd
Hermes House, 88–89 Blackfriars Road
London SE1 8HA
tel. 020 7401 2077; fax 020 7633 9499
www.southwaterbooks.com; info@anness.com

UK agent: The Manning Partnership Ltd
tel. 01225 478444; fax 01225 478440
sales@manning-partnership.co.uk

UK distributor: Grantham Book Services Ltd
tel. 01476 541080; fax 01476 541061
orders@gbs.tbs-ltd.co.uk

North American agent/distributor:
National Book Network
tel. 301 459 3366; fax 301 429 5746
www.nbnbooks.com

Australian agent/distributor: Pan Macmillan Australia
tel. 1300 135 113; fax 1300 135 103
customer.service@macmillan.com.au

New Zealand agent/distributor: David Bateman Ltd
tel. (09) 415 7664; fax (09) 415 8892

Publisher: Joanna Lorenz
Editorial Director: Helen Sudell
Editors: Nicola Baxter, Nicole Pearson,
Elizabeth Woodland and Joy Wotton
Designers: Simon Borrough and Margaret Sadler
Cover Designer: Sarah Williams
Illustrators: Robert Ashby, Vanessa Card, Stuart Carter,
Shane Marsh, Rob Sheffield and Clive Spong
Photography: John Freeman
Picture Researchers: Carrie Haines and Sarah Hopper
Stylists: Thomasina Smith and Melanie Williams
Production Controller: Claire Rae

Oakes, Lorna

Everyday life
in ancient
Egypt &

J932

1619057

Previously published in two separate volumes,
Step Into Ancient Egypt and *Step Into Mesopotamia*

10 9 8 7 6 5 4 3 2 1

CONTENTS

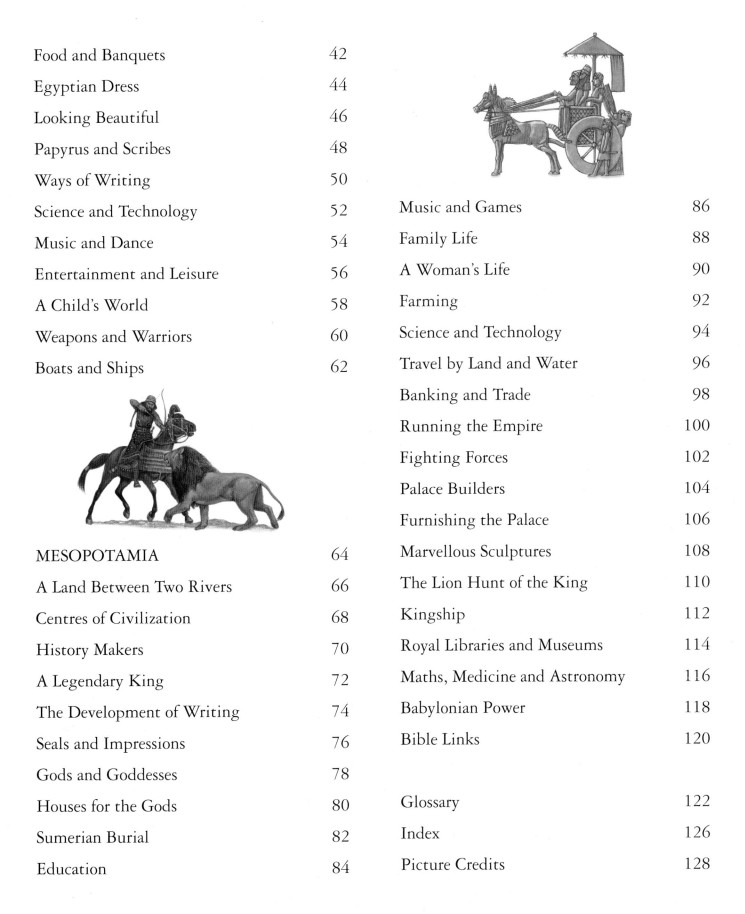

Introduction

J ourney into the past and discover the amazing civilizations of Egypt and Mesopotamia. This fact-filled project book brings to life the fascinating story of these people who lived thousands of years ago. You will find out what everyday life was like, about the governments and laws, their beliefs, how they studied science and used technology.

CARVED IN STONE
Early forms of writing, known as hieroglyphics, and pictures carved in stone, give a fascinating insight into Egypt's ancient civilization.

THE GREAT EMPIRES
In ancient Egypt, about 8,000 years ago, one of the greatest and longest lasting civilizations began when people settled in the Nile Valley and started to plant crops and raise animals. Walled towns were being built in Egypt from about 3400BC. A great civilization had developed there by 2686BC and it lasted for much of the next two thousand years, before being swallowed up by Assyrian, Persian, Greek and Roman invaders. Ancient Egypt was the land of the huge pointed tombs called pyramids, of the powerful rulers we call pharaohs, of massive temples and sculptures, of craftsmanship, painting and trade.

In the region that we now call the Middle East, the most important rivers were the Tigris and the Euphrates, which flowed through the land now known as Iraq. This area became known by a Greek name, "Mesopotamia" – meaning "the land between the rivers". This book tells the story of these great empires that came to power and then declined, of the Egyptians, and the Middle Eastern peoples known as Elamites, Amorites, Kassites, Assyrians and Persians. We learn of the rise and fall of splendid cities such as Babylon and of massive temple mounds called ziggurats, which towered to the sky.

ANIMAL HELPERS
The taming of wild animals helped humans in many ways, providing food, wool, hides (skins) and milk. Egyptian farmers were using donkeys at least 5,000 years ago, and horses were first introduced into Egypt from western Asia about 4,000 years ago. They were used to pull chariots, for warfare or hunting.

BESIDE THE TIGRIS
Rivers made it possible to irrigate crops. They also provided water for drinking and routes for shipping. The city of Nimrud was a late Assyrian capital, built in Mesopotamia on the east bank of the river Tigris in 879BC.

FERTILE LANDS

Farming became a way of life in Mesopotamia around 7000BC. Soon villages and then towns were being built of mud bricks. Pottery, textiles and copper goods were being produced. After 3000BC a people called the Sumerians founded cities, which were ruled by kings. A ruler called Sargon of Agade, who came to the throne in 2334BC, founded the world's first empire, by subjecting other cities to his rule. The lands of the Middle East were more fertile in ancient times, before a changing climate caused the spread of deserts. A "fertile crescent", a great arc of land suitable for farming, stretched from Mesopotamia towards what is now southern Turkey and the lands of the eastern Mediterranean. To the west, another long river, the Nile, flowed through the deserts of North Africa, before forming a green delta on the Mediterranean coast.

ZIGGURAT
The ziggurat was a common feature of Mesopotamian cities. It was a huge multi-storeyed brick mound, pointing to the heavens. On the top was a temple to the god or goddess who was believed to protect the city.

THE FIRST FARMERS

Agriculture first occurred in places where the climate was suitable and the ground was fertile. River valleys were ideal, where annual floods left behind rich mud in which to grow barley or other grain crops. The water of the rivers could be channelled into drier areas, for irrigating crops. Civilizations developed separately and at different times in various parts of the world. They grew up at times of change, when people were beginning to live by raising sheep or cattle or growing crops, instead of by hunting and following herds of wild animals. With a guaranteed supply of food and water, people could remain in the same place all year round. They could build towns and surround them with walls to keep out their enemies.

A LIFELIFE
The river Nile was a lifeline for the civilization of ancient Egypt. Each year its floods deposited thick mud on the river banks, forming good agricultural soil. Priests drew up calendars to predict the times of floods, sowing and harvests.

GARDENS IN THE SKY
Greek travellers writing about 2,300 years ago recorded that ancient Babylon was famous for its irrigated terraces of plants and trees, the so-called "hanging gardens". It was said these had been built by King Nebuchadnezzar II (604–562BC), for his wife. The location of the gardens is unknown.

UNCOVERING HISTORY

How do we know about all these ancient civilizations? There are of course references to them in ancient literature that has survived, and in scriptures such as the Bible. Since the nineteenth century, all sorts of discoveries have been made by archaeologists and scholars. They have unearthed impressive monuments, statues and tombs. They have decoded ancient languages and scripts. They have brought to light everyday items which remind us that the Mesopotamians and the Egyptians were people like us. In tombs, archaeologists have discovered jewellery, musical instruments, board games, clothes, toys and pictures. By examining the bodies of ancient Egyptians, archaeologists have found out what people ate in those days, what illnesses they suffered from, and how long they lived.

POWER OF THE PHARAOHS
The great temple of Abu Simbel in southern Egypt is dominated by vast statues of the pharaoh Ramesses II, who died in 1213BC. In the ancient world, rulers had great personal power.

Many archaeological discoveries, such as the amazing discovery of the treasure-filled tomb of the young pharaoh Tutankhamun in middle Egypt, have captured the public imagination in modern times. If one travels to the Middle East or Egypt one can see many such ancient remains. However, many fabulous treasures may also be seen in great museums and galleries around the world, from Europe to the United States. If you do not live near such a museum, you can still view these treasures in books or on the internet.

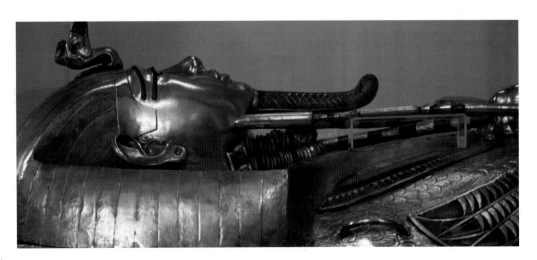

A FUNERAL PROCESSION
About 4,500 years ago, a Sumerian funeral procession may have looked like this. Ancient peoples often left offerings to the gods or personal belongings in tombs, so they are of particular interest to archaeologists.

THE GOLDEN PHARAOH
In 1922 archaeologist Howard Carter opened up the tomb of the Egyptian pharaoh Tutankhamun, who had died in 1325BC. Treasures such as this golden coffin case made this archaeological dig the most famous of all time.

Learning from the Past

The achievements of ancient Mesopotamia and Egypt are not just interesting in themselves. They are important because they changed the course of human history and affect our lives today. In agriculture, technology, transport, building, arts, crafts and social organization, the modern developments which we take for granted are rooted in those of the past.

As you read this book, remember that some of the earliest examples of writing in the world are symbols pressed into clay tablets by the Sumerians. As you read or hear about a legal trial or a new law, remember that a collection of laws was written down on stone for Hammurabi, ruler of Babylon, over 3,750 years ago. Next time you see a giant crane on a building site, remember that the Great Pyramid at Giza, tomb of the pharaoh Khufu in 2566BC, was for countless generations the biggest building in the world. It was built by hand, without cranes or bulldozers, and yet it still stands today. As you eat a piece of bread, remember the first grain grown by farmers of the ancient world, and also the people who ground it into flour and baked it in their ovens. As you look at your watch, have you wondered why there are 60 minutes in an hour? The answer lies with the Sumerians.

The Egyptians used to preserve the bodies of the dead as mummies, so that they could live for ever in the afterlife. In fact the ancient Egyptians and indeed the Mesopotamians have achieved another kind of immortality, because thousands of years later we are still fascinated by these ancient civilizations and impressed by their achievements.

Visiting the Temple
Tourists in middle Egypt can visit the temple which commemorates Hatshepsut, a female pharaoh who ruled from 1498 to 1483BC. Women rarely ruled in their own right in the ancient world.

Mythical Beast
This huge creature was part human, part bird and part animal. Its statue was sited at the entrance to Assyrian palaces to guard against evil spirits.

Everlasting Life
The ankh was an emblem of life in ancient Egypt. In many temples there are reliefs depicting the gods handing over the ankh to a pharaoh, showing that the ruler was given life by the gods.

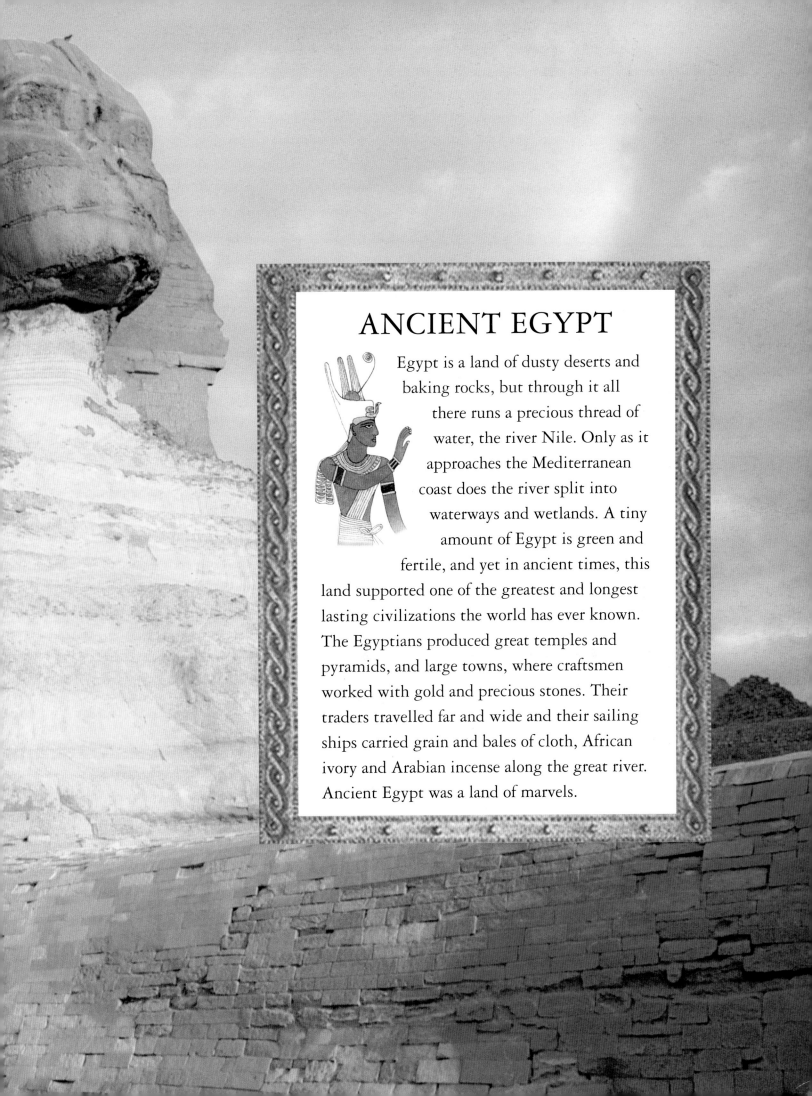

ANCIENT EGYPT

Egypt is a land of dusty deserts and baking rocks, but through it all there runs a precious thread of water, the river Nile. Only as it approaches the Mediterranean coast does the river split into waterways and wetlands. A tiny amount of Egypt is green and fertile, and yet in ancient times, this land supported one of the greatest and longest lasting civilizations the world has ever known. The Egyptians produced great temples and pyramids, and large towns, where craftsmen worked with gold and precious stones. Their traders travelled far and wide and their sailing ships carried grain and bales of cloth, African ivory and Arabian incense along the great river. Ancient Egypt was a land of marvels.

The Kingdom on the Nile

EGYPT IS A COUNTRY at the crossroads of Africa, Europe and Asia. If you could step back in time 5,000 years, you would discover an amazing civilization – the kingdom of the ancient Egyptians.

Most of Egypt is made up of baking hot, sandy deserts. These are crossed by the river Nile as it snakes its way north to the Mediterranean Sea. Every year, floods cover the banks of the Nile with mud. Plants grow well in this rich soil, and 8,000 years ago farmers were planting crops here. Wealth from farming led to trade and to the building of towns. By 3100BC a great kingdom had grown up in Egypt, ruled by royal families.

Ancient Egypt existed for over 3,000 years, longer even than the Roman Empire. Pyramids, temples and artefacts survive from this period to show us what life was like in the land of the pharaohs.

HORUS' EYE
This symbol can be seen on many Egyptian artefacts. It is the eye of the god Horus.

AMAZING DISCOVERIES
In 1922, the English archaeologist Howard Carter made an amazing discovery. He found the tomb of the young pharaoh Tutankhamun. No single find in Egypt has ever provided as much evidence as the discovery of this well-preserved tomb.

LIFE BY THE NILE
Tomb paintings show us how people lived in ancient Egypt. Here people water and harvest their crops, using water from the river Nile.

TIMELINE 6000BC–2000BC

The kingdom of ancient Egypt existed for over 3,000 years. The most successful periods of Egyptian power are known as the Old Kingdom, the Middle Kingdom and the New Kingdom.

wheat

sheep

boat with sail

c6000BC
Early people settle in the fertile Nile valley. They grow wheat and barley.

c5020–4500BC
Craftsmen make clay figures and fine pottery vessels. They also carve objects from ivory.

c4800BC
Farmers keep sheep, cattle and other animals.

c4000BC
Sails are used on Egyptian ships for the first time.

6000BC	5500BC	5000BC	4500BC	4000BC

THE KINGDOM OF EGYPT

This map of Egypt today shows where there were important cities and sites in ancient times. The ancient Egyptians lived mostly along the banks of the river Nile and in the green, fertile lands of the delta. Through the ages, the Egyptians built many imposing temples in honour of their gods and mysterious tombs to house their dead. Most of these temples and tombs were built close to the major cities of Memphis and Thebes.

SURVIVORS OF THE DESERT

The face of the great pharaoh Ramesses II stares out at us. Huge statues of Ramesses were part of a temple cut from the rock face at Abu Simbel in 1269BC. During the 1960s the statues had to be raised because a new dam at Aswan turned this part of the Nile into a lake. Temples, tombs and statues such as those at Abu Simbel have survived for thousands of years in the dry desert heat. More recently, many monuments have started to disintegrate because of the polluted air around modern cities such as Luxor.

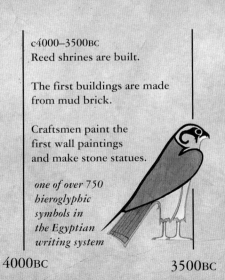

c4000–3500BC Reed shrines are built.

The first buildings are made from mud brick.

Craftsmen paint the first wall paintings and make stone statues.

one of over 750 hieroglyphic symbols in the Egyptian writing system

c3400BC Walled towns are built in Egypt.

3100BC The first of the great royal families govern Egypt. The Early Dynastic period begins.

King Narmer unites Egypt. He creates a capital at Memphis.

Egyptians use hieroglyphs.

2686BC Old Kingdom period.

2667BC Zoser becomes pharaoh.

2650BC Stepped pyramid built at Saqqara.

Stepped Pyramid

2600BC Pyramid built at Maidum.

2589BC Khufu becomes pharaoh. He later builds the Great Pyramid at Giza.

Great Sphinx

c2500BC Khafra, son of Khufu, dies. During his reign the Great Sphinx was.built at Giza.

2181BC The Old Kingdom comes to an end.

The Intermediate Period begins. Minor kings in power.

4000BC   3500BC   3000BC   2500BC   2000BC

A Great Civilization

THE STORY of ancient Egypt began about 8,000 years ago when farmers started to plant crops and raise animals in the Nile Valley. By about 3400BC the Egyptians were building walled towns. Soon after that the northern part of the country (Lower Egypt) was united with the lands upstream (Upper Egypt) to form one country under a single king. The capital of this new kingdom was established at Memphis.

The first great period of Egyptian civilization is called the Old Kingdom. It lasted from 2686BC to 2181BC. This was when the pharaohs built great pyramids, the massive pointed tombs that still stand in the desert today.

During the Middle Kingdom (2050–1786BC), the capital was moved to the southern city of Thebes. The Egyptians gained control of Nubia and extended the area of land being farmed. Despite this period of success, the rule of the royal families of ancient Egypt was sometimes interrupted by disorder. In 1663BC, control of the country fell into foreign hands. The Hyksos, a group of Asian settlers, ruled Egypt for almost 100 years.

In 1567BC the Hyksos were overthrown by the princes of Thebes. The Thebans established the New Kingdom. This was the highest point of Egyptian civilization. Traders and soldiers travelled into Africa, Asia and the lands of the Mediterranean. However, by 525BC, the might of the Egyptians was coming to an end and Egypt became part of the Persian Empire. In 332BC rule passed to the Greeks. Finally, in 30BC, conquest was complete as Egypt fell under the control of the Roman Empire.

AFRICA

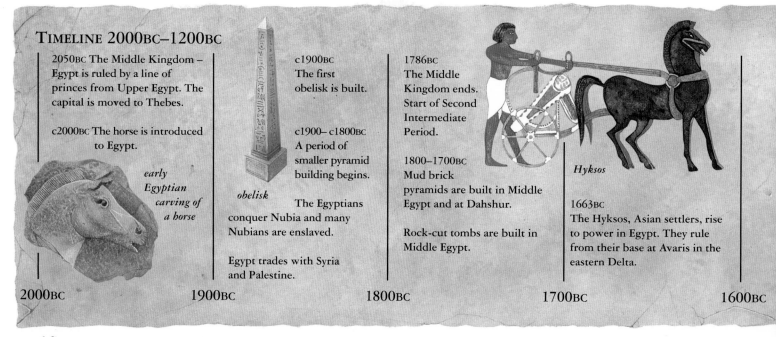

TIMELINE 2000BC–1200BC

2050BC The Middle Kingdom – Egypt is ruled by a line of princes from Upper Egypt. The capital is moved to Thebes.

c2000BC The horse is introduced to Egypt.

early Egyptian carving of a horse

c1900BC The first obelisk is built.

obelisk

c1900– c1800BC A period of smaller pyramid building begins.

The Egyptians conquer Nubia and many Nubians are enslaved.

Egypt trades with Syria and Palestine.

1786BC The Middle Kingdom ends. Start of Second Intermediate Period.

1800–1700BC Mud brick pyramids are built in Middle Egypt and at Dahshur.

Rock-cut tombs are built in Middle Egypt.

Hyksos

1663BC The Hyksos, Asian settlers, rise to power in Egypt. They rule from their base at Avaris in the eastern Delta.

| 2000BC | 1900BC | 1800BC | 1700BC | 1600BC |

EUROPE

naean Empire

Hittite Empire

Kadesh battle site

MINOAN CRETE

Mediterranean Sea

Byblos.

LEVANT

Megiddo.

Jerusalem.

. Avaris

LOWER EGYPT

Memphis Sinai

EGYPT

River Nile

Western Desert

Thebes.

UPPER
EGYPT

NUBIA

Red Sea

SYRIA

PALESTINE

ARABIA

NORTH

ASIA

MESOPOTAMIA

MAP OF THE NEAR EAST
In 1279BC, at the height of
the New Kingdom,
Egypt was a leading
power in the Near
East. The country was
prosperous and rich, trading with
Minoan Crete, Syria, the Levant and
Nubia. Nevertheless, it faced threats
from enemies such as the Hittites.

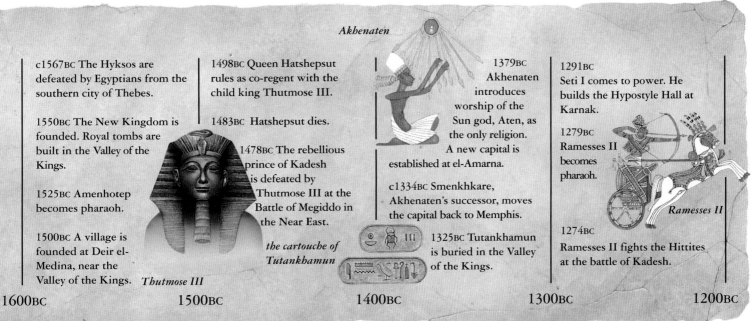

Akhenaten

c1567BC The Hyksos are
defeated by Egyptians from the
southern city of Thebes.

1550BC The New Kingdom is
founded. Royal tombs are
built in the Valley of the
Kings.

1525BC Amenhotep
becomes pharaoh.

1500BC A village is
founded at Deir el-
Medina, near the
Valley of the Kings.

Thutmose III

1498BC Queen Hatshepsut
rules as co-regent with the
child king Thutmose III.

1483BC Hatshepsut dies.

1478BC The rebellious
prince of Kadesh
is defeated by
Thutmose III at the
Battle of Megiddo in
the Near East.

*the cartouche of
Tutankhamun*

1379BC
Akhenaten
introduces
worship of the
Sun god, Aten, as
the only religion.
A new capital is
established at el-Amarna.

c1334BC Smenkhkare,
Akhenaten's successor, moves
the capital back to Memphis.

1325BC Tutankhamun
is buried in the Valley
of the Kings.

1291BC
Seti I comes to power. He
builds the Hypostyle Hall at
Karnak.

1279BC
Ramesses II
becomes
pharaoh.

Ramesses II

1274BC
Ramesses II fights the Hittites
at the battle of Kadesh.

1600BC   1500BC   1400BC   1300BC   1200BC

Famous Pharaohs

FOR THOUSANDS OF YEARS ancient Egypt was ruled by royal families. We know much about the pharaohs and queens from these great dynasties because of their magnificent tombs and the public monuments raised in their honour.

Egypt's first ruler was King Narmer, who united the country in about 3100BC. Later pharaohs such as Zoser and Khufu are remembered for the great pyramids they had built as their tombs.

Pharaohs usually succeeded to the throne through royal birth. However, in some cases military commanders such as Horemheb came to power. Although Egypt's rulers were traditionally men, a few powerful women were made pharaoh. The most famous of these is the Greek queen Cleopatra, who ruled Egypt in 51BC.

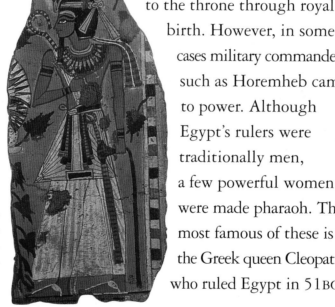

KHAFRA
(reigned 2558–2532BC)
Khafra is the son of the pharaoh Khufu. He is remembered for his splendid tomb, the Second Pyramid at Giza and the Great Sphinx that guards it.

AMENHOTEP I
(reigned 1525–1504BC)
The pharaoh Amenhotep led the Egyptian army to battle in Nubia. He also founded the workmen's village at Deir el-Medina.

HATSHEPSUT
(reigned 1498–1483BC)
Hatshepsut was the half-sister and wife of Thutmose II. When her husband died, she was appointed to rule Egypt until her young stepson Thutmose III was old enough. However Queen Hatshepsut was ambitious and had herself crowned pharaoh. Hatshepsut is famous for her trading expeditions to the land of Punt. The walls of her temple at Deir el-Bahri show these exotic trips.

TIMELINE 1200BC–AD1960

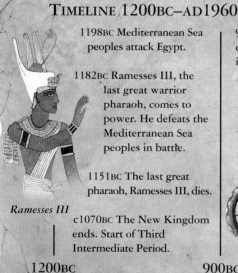

1198BC Mediterranean Sea peoples attack Egypt.

1182BC Ramesses III, the last great warrior pharaoh, comes to power. He defeats the Mediterranean Sea peoples in battle.

1151BC The last great pharaoh, Ramesses III, dies.

Ramesses III

c1070BC The New Kingdom ends. Start of Third Intermediate Period.

900–700BC Brief periods of calm between conquest by invading armies.

671BC Assyrians conquer Egypt as far as Memphis.

Darius I

525BC Beginning of the Late Dynastic Period.

525BC Egypt becomes part of the Persian Empire.

332BC Egypt is invaded by Alexander the Great and is ruled by Greek kings. Alexandria is built. *Alexander the Great*

305BC Ptolemy I, a commander in Alexander the Great's army, takes power after his death.

51BC Cleopatra VII, Ptolemy's XII's daughter, reigns in Egypt.

Cleopatra VII

30BC Egypt becomes part of the Roman Empire under the emperor Augustus.

| 1200BC | 900BC | 600BC | 300BC | AD0 |

TUTANKHAMUN
(reigned 1334–1325BC)
This pharaoh came to the throne when he was only nine years old. He died at the age of 18. Tutankhamun is remembered for his tomb in the Valley of the Kings, which was packed with amazing treasure.

THUTMOSE III
(reigned 1479–1425BC)
Thutmose III is remembered as a brave warrior king. He launched many military campaigns against the Syrians in the Near East. Records from the time tell of Thutmose marching fearlessly into battle at the head of his army, unconcerned about his own safety. He won a famous victory at Megiddo and then later at Kadesh. Thutmose III was buried in the Valley of the Kings.

AKHENATEN
(reigned 1379–1334BC)
The Egyptians believed in many gods. However, when Akhenaten came to power, he introduced worship of one god, the Sun disc Aten. He moved the capital from Memphis to Akhetaten (now known as el-Amarna). His chief wife was the beautiful Queen Nefertiti.

RAMESSES II
(reigned 1279–1212BC)
One of the most famous pharaohs of all, Ramesses II, was the son of Seti I. He built many fine temples and defeated the Hittites at the Battle of Kadesh in 1274BC. The chief queen of Ramesses was Nefertari. Carvings of this graceful queen can be seen on Ramesses II's temple at Abu Simbel. Ramesses lived a long life and died at the age of 92. He was buried in the Valley of the Kings.

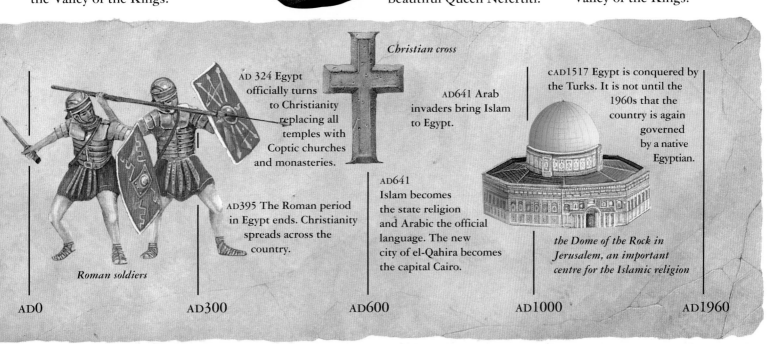

Christian cross

AD 324 Egypt officially turns to Christianity replacing all temples with Coptic churches and monasteries.

AD641 Arab invaders bring Islam to Egypt.

cAD1517 Egypt is conquered by the Turks. It is not until the 1960s that the country is again governed by a native Egyptian.

AD395 The Roman period in Egypt ends. Christianity spreads across the country.

AD641 Islam becomes the state religion and Arabic the official language. The new city of el-Qahira becomes the capital Cairo.

Roman soldiers

the Dome of the Rock in Jerusalem, an important centre for the Islamic religion

| AD0 | AD300 | AD600 | AD1000 | AD1960 |

The Land of the Gods

THE ANCIENT EGYPTIANS believed that the ordered world in which they lived had been created out of nothingness. Chaos and darkness could return at any time if the proper religious rituals were not followed. The spirit of the gods lived inside the pharaohs, who were honoured as god-kings. They looked after the everyday world for the gods. Over 2,000 gods were worshipped in ancient Egypt. Many gods were linked to a particular region. The mighty Amun was the god of Thebes. Some gods appeared as animals – Sebek the water god was a crocodile. Gods were also connected with jobs and interests. The hippopotamus goddess, Tawaret, looked after babies and childbirth.

Many ordinary Egyptians understood little about the religion of the court and nobles. They believed in magic, local spirits and superstitions.

HORUS
Horus the falcon god was the son of Isis. He was god of the sky and protector of the reigning pharaoh. The name Horus meant "He who is far above". Here he holds an *ankh*, the symbol of life. The holder of an *ankh* had the power to give life or take it away. Only pharaohs and gods were allowed to carry them.

LOTUS FLOWER
The lotus was a very important flower to the Egyptians. This sacred symbol was used to represent Upper Egypt.

THE GODDESS NUT
Nut, covered in stars, was goddess of the heavens. She is often shown with her body stretched across the sky. The Egyptians believed that Nut swallowed the Sun each evening and gave birth to it the next morning. She was married to the Earth god, Geb, and gave birth to the gods Isis and Osiris.

AMUN OF THEBES

Amun was originally the god of the city of Thebes. He later became popular throughout Egypt as the god of creation. By the time of the New Kingdom, Amun was combined with other powerful gods such as Ra, god of the Sun, and became known as Amun-Ra. He was believed to be the most powerful god of all. Amun is sometimes shown as a ram.

HOLY BEETLES

Scarabs are beetles that were sacred to the ancient Egyptians. Pottery or stone scarabs were used as lucky charms, seals, or as ring decorations. The base of these scarabs was often inscribed with stories telling of some great event.

OSIRIS, KING OF THE UNDERWORLD

The great god Osiris stands dressed as a king. He was one of the most important gods in ancient Egypt, the master of life and the spirit world. He was also the god of farming. Egyptian tales told how Osiris was murdered and cut into pieces by his brother Seth, the god of chaos. Anubis, the jackal-headed god of embalming, gathered the pieces together and his sister, Isis, brought Osiris back to life.

CAT MUMMIES

The Egyptians worshipped gods in the forms of animals from the Old Kingdom onwards. The cat goddess Bastet was said to be the daughter of the great Sun god, Ra. Cats were so holy to the Egyptians that at one time many of them were embalmed, wrapped in linen bandages and preserved as mummies. It is thought that bronze cat figures and these mummified cats were left as offerings to Bastet at her temple.

MIW THE CAT

Cats were holy animals in ancient Egypt. They even had their own god! The Egyptians' love of cats dated back to the early farmers who tamed cats to protect stores of grain from mice. Cats soon became popular pets. The Egyptian word for cat was *miw*, which was rather like a mew or miaow!

Priest, Politician and God

T HE WORD PHARAOH comes from the Egyptian *per-aa*, which meant great house or palace. It later came to mean the man who lived in the palace, the ruler. Pictures and statues show pharaohs with special badges of royalty, such as crowns, headcloths, false beards, sceptres and a crook and flail held in each hand.

The pharaoh was the most important person in Egypt. As a god-ruler, he was the link between the people and their gods. He therefore had to be protected and cared for. The pharaoh led a busy life. He was the high priest, the chief law-maker, the commander of the army and in charge of the country's wealth. He had to be a clever politician, too. The ancient Egyptians believed that on his death, the pharaoh became a god in his own right.

Pharaohs were generally men, but queens sometimes ruled Egypt if the pharaoh was too young. A pharaoh could take several wives. Within royal families it was common for fathers to marry daughters and for brothers to marry sisters. Sometimes pharaohs married foreign princesses in order to make an alliance with another country.

THE CROOK AND FLAIL
These emblems of the god Osiris became badges of royal authority. The crook stood for kingship and the flail for the fertility of the land.

flail

crook

MOTHER GODDESS OF THE PHARAOHS
Hathor was worshipped as the mother goddess of each pharaoh. Here she is shown welcoming the pharaoh Horemheb to the afterlife. Horemheb was a nobleman who became a brilliant military commander. He was made pharaoh in 1323BC.

MAKE A CROWN

You will need: 2 sheets of A1 card (red and white), pencil, ruler, scissors, masking tape, cardboard roll, bandage, pva glue and brush, acrylic paint (white, gold), brush, beads, skewer, water pot and brush.

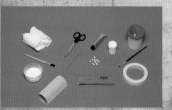

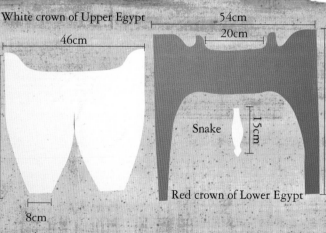

White crown of Upper Egypt

46cm

40cm

8cm

54cm

20cm

Snake

15cm

55cm

Red crown of Lower Egypt

Mark out these patterns onto your card. Cut around them with scissors.

1 Bend the shape made from the white card into a cylinder, as shown. Use lengths of masking tape to join the two edges together firmly.

RAMESSES MEETS THE GODS

This painting shows the dead pharaoh Ramesses I meeting the gods Horus (left) and Anubis (right). Pharaohs had to pass safely through the after-life or the link between the gods and the world would be broken forever.

THE QUEEN'S TEMPLE

This great temple (*below*) was built in honour of Queen Hatshepsut. It lies at the foot of towering cliffs at Deir el-Bahri, on the west bank of the Nile near the Valley of the Kings. The queen had the temple built as a place for her body to be prepared for burial. Pyramids, tombs and temples were important symbols of power in Egypt. By building this temple, Hatshepsut wanted people to remember her as a pharaoh in her own right.

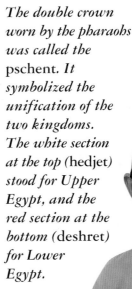

HATSHEPSUT

A female pharaoh was so unusual that pictures of Queen Hatshepsut show her with all the badges of a male king, including a false beard! Here she wears the pharaoh's crown. The cobra on the front of the crown is the badge of Lower Egypt.

The double crown worn by the pharaohs was called the pschent. *It symbolized the unification of the two kingdoms. The white section at the top* (hedjet) *stood for Upper Egypt, and the red section at the bottom* (deshret) *for Lower Egypt.*

2 Tape a cardboard roll into the hole at the top. Plug its end with a ball of bandage. Then tape the bandage in position and glue down the edges.

3 Wrap the white section with lengths of bandage. Paint over these with an equal mixture of white paint and glue. Leave the crown in a warm place to dry.

4 Now take the shape made from the red card. Wrap it tightly around the white section, as shown, joining the edges with masking tape.

5 Now paint the snake gold, sticking on beads as eyes. When dry, score lines across its body. Bend the snake's body and glue it to the crown, as shown.

19

Court and Nobles

EGYPTIAN PALACES were vast complexes. They included splendid public buildings where the pharaoh would meet foreign rulers and carry out important ceremonies. Members of the royal family lived in luxury in beautiful townhouses with painted walls and tiled floors near the palace.

The governors of Egypt's regions also lived like princes, and pharaohs had to be careful that they did not become too rich and powerful. The royal court included large numbers of officials and royal advisors. There were lawyers, architects, tax officials, priests and army officers. The most important court official of all was the vizier, who carried out many of the pharaoh's duties for him.

The officials and nobles were at the top of Egyptian society. But most of the hard work that kept the country running smoothly was carried out by merchants and craft workers, by farmers, labourers and slaves.

GREAT LADIES
Ahmose-Nefertari was the wife of Ahmose I. She carries a lotus flower and a flail. Kings could take many wives and it was also common for them to have a harem of beautiful women.

A NOBLEMAN AND HIS WIFE
This limestone statue shows an unknown couple from Thebes. The man may have worked in a well-respected profession, as a doctor, government official, or engineer. Noblewomen did not work but were quite independent. Any property that a wife brought into her marriage remained hers.

THE SPLENDOURS OF THE COURT
This is the throne room of Ramesses III's palace at Medinet Habu, on the west bank of the Nile near Thebes. Pharaohs often had many palaces and Medinet Habu was one of Ramesses III's lesser ones. Surviving fragments of tiles and furniture give us an idea of just how splendid the royal court must have been. A chamber to one side of the throne room is even believed to be an early version of a shower cubicle!

RELAXATION

Ankherhau (*above*), a wealthy overseer of workmen, relaxes at home with his wife. They are listening to a harpist. Life was pleasant for those who could afford it. Kings and nobles had dancers, musicians and acrobats to entertain them. Cooks worked in their kitchens preparing sumptuous meals. By comparison, ordinary people ate simple food, rarely eating meat except for the small animals they caught themselves.

HAIR CARE

The royal family was waited on by domestic servants who attended to their every need. Here (*left*), the young Queen Kawit, wife of the pharaoh Mentuhotep II, has her hair dressed by her personal maid. Although many of the female servants employed in wealthy households were slaves, a large number of servants were free. This meant that they had the right to leave their employer at any time.

Towns, Homes and Gardens

THE GREAT CITIES of ancient Egypt, such as Memphis and Thebes, were built along the banks of the river Nile. Small towns grew up haphazardly around them. Special workmen's towns such as Deir el-Medina were also set up around major burial sites and temples to help with building work.

Egyptian towns were defended by thick walls and the streets were planned on a grid pattern. The straight dirt roads had a stone drainage channel, or gutter, running down the middle. Parts of the town housed important officials, while other parts were home to craft workers and poor labourers.

Only temples were built to last. They were made of stone. Mud brick was used to construct all other buildings from royal palaces to workers' dwellings. Most Egyptian homes had roofs supported with palm logs and floors made of packed earth. In the homes of wealthier Egyptians, walls were sometimes plastered and painted. The rooms of their houses included bedrooms, living rooms, kitchens in thatched courtyards and workshops. Homes were furnished with beds, chairs, stools and benches. In the cool of the evenings people would sit on the flat roofs or walk and talk in cool, shady gardens.

THE GARDEN OF NAKHT
The royal scribe Nakht and his wife Tjiui take an evening stroll through their garden. Trees and shrubs surround a peaceful pool. Egyptian gardens included date palms, pomegranates, grape vines, scarlet poppies and blue and pink lotus flowers. Artists in ancient Egypt showed objects in the same picture from different angles, so the trees around Nakht's pool are flattened out.

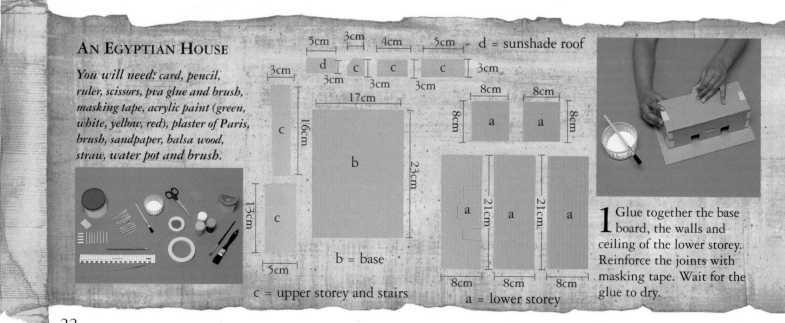

AN EGYPTIAN HOUSE

You will need: card, pencil, ruler, scissors, pva glue and brush, masking tape, acrylic paint (green, white, yellow, red), plaster of Paris, brush, sandpaper, balsa wood, straw, water pot and brush.

d = sunshade roof

b = base

c = upper storey and stairs

a = lower storey

1 Glue together the base board, the walls and ceiling of the lower storey. Reinforce the joints with masking tape. Wait for the glue to dry.

22

ABOVE THE FLOODS

The homes of wealthy people were often built on platforms to stop damp passing through the mud brick walls. This also raised it above the level of any possible flood damage.

SOUL HOUSES

Pottery models give us a good idea of how the homes of poorer Egyptians looked. During the Middle Kingdom, these soul houses were left as tomb offerings. The Egyptians placed food in the courtyard of the house to feed the person's soul after death.

MUD BRICK

The Egyptians made mud bricks from the thick clay soil left behind by the Nile floods. The clay was taken to the brickyard and mixed with water, pebbles and chopped straw. Mud brick is still used as a building material for houses in Egypt today and is made in the same way.

straw

mud

BRICK MAKING

A group of labourers make bricks. First mud was collected in leather buckets and taken to the building site. There, it was mixed with straw and pebbles. Finally the mixture was put into a mould. At this stage, bricks were sometimes stamped with the name of the pharaoh or the building for which they were made. They were then left to dry in the hot sunshine for several days, before being carried away in a sling.

Egyptian houses had a large main room that opened directly onto the street. In many homes, stairs led up to the roof. People would often sleep there during very hot weather.

2 Now glue together the top storey and stairs. Again, use masking tape to reinforce the joints. When the top storey is dry, glue it to the lower storey.

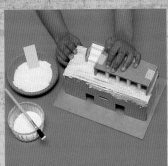

3 Glue the balsa pillars into the front of the top storey. When the house is dry, cover it in wet paste of plaster of Paris. Paint the pillars red or a colour of your choice.

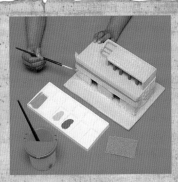

4 Paint the whole building a dried mud colour. Next paint a green strip along the side. Use masking tape to ensure straight edges. Sand any rough edges.

5 Now make a shelter for the rooftop. Use four balsa struts as supports. The roof can be made of card glued with straw. Glue the shelter into place.

Arts and Crafts

ALABASTER ART
This elaborate jar was among the treasures in the tomb of Tutankhamun. Jars such as this would have held precious oils and perfumes.

THE ANCIENT EGYPTIANS loved beautiful objects, and the craft items that have survived still amaze us today. There are shining gold rings and pendants, necklaces inlaid with glass and a dazzling blue pottery called faience. Jars made of a smooth white stone called alabaster have been preserved in almost perfect condition, along with chairs and chests made of cedar wood imported from the Near East.

Egyptians made beautiful baskets and storage pots. Some pottery was made from river clay, but the finest pots were made from a chalky clay found at Quena. Pots were shaped by hand or, later, on a potter's wheel. Some were polished with a smooth pebble until their surface shone. We know so much about Egyptian craft work because many beautiful items were placed in tombs, so that the dead person could use them in the next world.

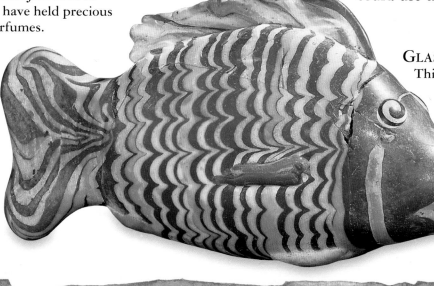

GLASS FISH
This beautiful stripy fish looks as if it should be swimming in the reefs of the Red Sea. In fact it is a glass jar used to store oils. Glass-making became popular in Egypt after 1500BC. The glass was made from sand and salty crystals. It would then have been coloured with metals and shaped while still hot.

MAKE A LOTUS TILE

You will need: card (2 sheets), pencil, ruler, scissors, self-drying clay, modelling tool, sandpaper acrylic paint (blue, gold, green, yellow ochre), water pot and brush. Optional: rolling pin & board.

1 Using the final picture as reference, draw both tile shapes onto card. Cut them out. Draw the whole pattern of tiles onto the sheet of card and cut around the border.

2 Roll out the clay on a board with a rolling pin or bottle. Place the overall outline over the clay and carefully trim off the edges. Discard the extra clay.

3 Mark the individual tile patterns into the clay, following the outlines carefully. Cut through the lines, but do not separate them out yet.

DESERT RICHES

The dwellers of the green Nile valley feared and disliked the desert. They called it the Red Land. However, the deserts did provide them with great mineral wealth, including blue-green turquoise, purple amethyst and blue agate.

blue agate   *turquoise*   *amethyst*

ROYAL TILES

Many beautiful tiles have been discovered by archaeologists. It is thought that they were used to decorate furniture and floors in the palaces of the Egyptian pharaohs.

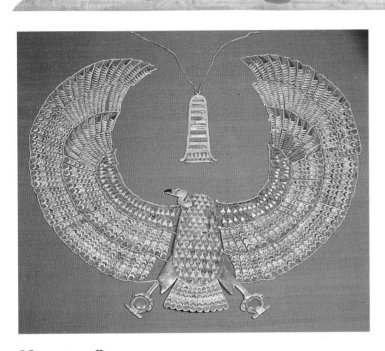

NEKHBET COLLAR

This splendid collar was one of 17 found in Tutankhamun's tomb. The spectacular wings of the vulture goddess Nekhbet include 250 feather sections made of coloured glass set in gold. The vulture's beak and eye are made from a black, volcanic glass called obsidian. This and other amazing objects found in the young king's tomb show us the incredible skill of Egyptian craftsmen.

TUTANKHAMUN'S WAR CHEST

This painted chest shows Tutankhamun in battle against the Syrians and the Nubians. On the lid, the young king is also seen hunting in the desert. The incredible detail of the painting shows that this was the work of a very skilled artist. When Tutankhamun's tomb was opened, the chest was found to contain children's clothes. The desert air was so dry that neither the wood, leather nor fabric had rotted.

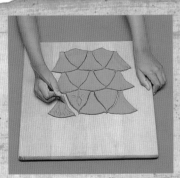

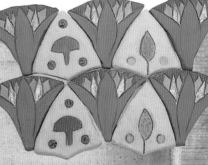

4 Now use the tool to score patterns of leaves and flowers into the surface of the soft clay, as shown. Separate the pieces and allow them to dry.

5 When one side of each tile has dried, turn it over. Leave the other side to dry. Then sand down the edges of the tiles until they are smooth.

6 The tiles are now ready for painting. Carefully paint the patterns in green, yellow ochre, gold and blue. Leave them in a warm place to dry.

These tiles are similar to those found at a royal palace in Thebes. The design looks rather like a lotus, the sacred waterlily of ancient Egypt.

The Pyramid Builders

THE PYRAMIDS were massive four-sided tombs, built for the pharaohs of the Old Kingdom. Each side, shaped like a triangle, met together in a point at the top. The first Egyptian pyramid was built at Saqqara in about 2650BC. It had stepped sides. The most impressive pyramids, built at Giza over 100 years later, had flat sides. The summit of each pyramid was probably capped in gold. Inside the pyramids were burial chambers and secret passages. No one really knows why the Egyptians built these tombs in pyramid shapes, but it may have been seen as a stairway to heaven to help the pharaoh achieve eternal life.

The pyramids were built with fantastic skill and mathematical accuracy by a team of architects, engineers and stonemasons. They still stand today. The manual labour was provided not by slaves, but by about 100,000 ordinary people. These unskilled workers had to offer their services each year when the flooding Nile made work in the fields impossible.

WORN DOWN BY THE WIND
This pyramid at Dahshur was built for pharaoh Amenemhat III. Once the limestone casing had been stolen, its mud-brick core was easily worn down by the harsh desert winds. Pyramids had become popular burial monuments after the building of the first step pyramid at Saqqara. Examples can be seen at Maidum, Dahshur and Giza. However, Amenemhat's pyramid is typical of those built during the Middle Kingdom when inferior materials were used.

THE STEP PYRAMID
The earliest step pyramid was built at Saqqara for the pharaoh Zoser. The tomb probably started out as a mastaba, an older type of burial site made up of a brick structure over an underground tomb. The upper levels of Zoser's mastaba were redesigned as a pyramid with six huge steps. It was 60m high and towered above the desert sands. It covered the underground tomb of the pharaoh and included 11 burial chambers for the other members of the royal family.

ROYAL ARCHITECT
Imhotep was vizier, or treasurer, in the court of the great pharaoh Zoser. He designed the huge step pyramid at Saqqara. This pyramid was the first large monument made entirely of stone. Imhotep was also a wise man who was an accomplished scribe, astronomer, doctor, priest and architect. In the late period of the Egyptian empire, he was worshipped as a god of medicine.

The Mysterious Sphinx

The pyramids of Giza are guarded by a huge sphinx. This massive stone statue of a lion has the head of a man, who may be the pharaoh Khafra. The Great Sphinx was probably built on Khafra's orders. It looks east, towards the rising Sun. For most of the last 4,500 years it has been covered in sand. An inscription on the Sphinx from 1419BC tells the story of Prince Thutmose IV who fell asleep between the statue's paws. The Sun god appeared to him and said that if he cleared the sand away from the Sphinx, he would be made king. This he did and he was then crowned pharaoh!

Nelson's Column

Sydney Opera House

Statue of Liberty

Great Pyramid

The Pyramids at Giza

The three pyramids of Giza belonged to the pharaoh Khufu, his son Khafra and the pharaoh Menkaura. Although Khafra's pyramid in the middle looks the largest of the three, it is actually built on slightly higher ground. Khufu's pyramid on the right, also known as the Great Pyramid, is the largest. In front of the large pyramids are three smaller structures that were built for the wives of Menkaura. When the pyramids were built they were covered in dazzling white limestone. Around the bottom of the pyramids a few of these original stone casing blocks can still be seen.

Scaling the Heights

The pyramids were, and still are, immense feats of architecture and engineering. When it was orginally built, the Great Pyramid was 147m tall. Even at its present height of 137m, it is larger than many more modern monuments.

The Third Pyramid
Original height: 70m

The Second Pyramid
Original height: 136m

The Great Pyramid
Original height: 147m

Wonder of the World

EARLY TOURISM
In the 1800s, many tourists climbed to the top of the Great Pyramid. From here, the best view of the Giza complex could be had. However, it was a dangerous climb and some visitors fell to their death.

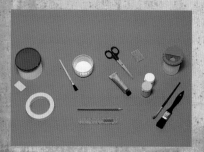

FOR MANY YEARS the Great Pyramid at Giza was the largest building in the world. Its base is about 230m square, and its original point was 147m high. It is made up of about 2,300,000 massive blocks of stone, each one weighing about 2.5 tonnes. It was the oldest of the seven ancient wonders of the world and is the only one left standing today. Even in ancient times, tourists came to marvel at the size of the Great Pyramid, and vast numbers of people still come to Giza today. The Great Pyramid is incredible in terms of both scale and age. It was built for the pharaoh Khufu, who died in 2566BC. Nearby was a great temple built in his honour. The purpose of the pyramid was to protect Khufu's body while he journeyed to meet the gods after his death. A 47m long passage leads to one of the three burial chambers inside the pyramid, but the pharaoh's body was never found in the tomb. It had been robbed long ago.

GRAND GALLERY
This steep passage is known as the Grand Gallery. It leads up to the burial chamber in the Great Pyramid. After King Khufu's funeral, granite blocks were slid down the gallery to seal off the chamber. However, ancient Egyptian tomb robbers still managed to break into the chamber and steal its contents.

MAKE A PYRAMID

You will need: card, pencil, ruler, scissors, pva glue and brush, masking tape, acrylic paint (yellow, white, gold), plaster paste, sandpaper, water pot and brush.

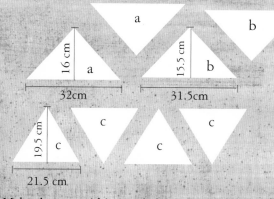

a
b
16 cm
a
15.5 cm
b
32cm
31.5cm
c
c
19.5 cm
c
c
21.5 cm

Make the pyramid in two halves. Cut out one triangle (a) for the base, one triangle (b) for the inside and two of triangle (c) for the sides of each half section.

1 Glue the half section of the pyramid together, binding the joints with pieces of masking tape, as shown. Now make the second half section in the same way.

INSIDE A PYRAMID

This cross-section shows the inside of the Great Pyramid. The design of the interior changed several times during its construction. An underground chamber may originally have been intended as Khufu's burial place. This chamber was never finished. A second chamber, known as the Queen's Chamber, was also found empty. The pharaoh was actually buried in the King's Chamber. Once the funeral was over, the tomb had to be sealed from the inside. Blocks of stone were slid down the Grand Gallery. The workmen left through a shaft and along a corridor before the stones thudded into place.

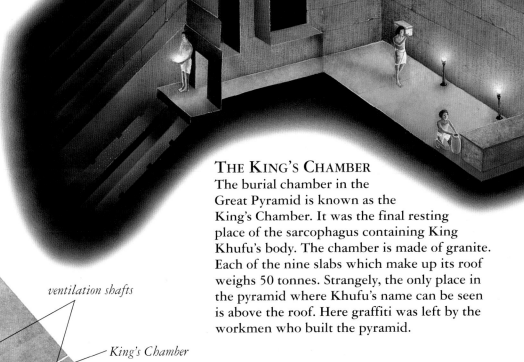

THE KING'S CHAMBER

The burial chamber in the Great Pyramid is known as the King's Chamber. It was the final resting place of the sarcophagus containing King Khufu's body. The chamber is made of granite. Each of the nine slabs which make up its roof weighs 50 tonnes. Strangely, the only place in the pyramid where Khufu's name can be seen is above the roof. Here graffiti was left by the workmen who built the pyramid.

ventilation shafts

King's Chamber

Grand Gallery

Queen's Chamber

escape shaft for workers

corridor

unfinished chamber

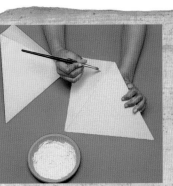

2 Mix up yellow and white paint with a little plaster paste to achieve a sandy texture. Then add a little glue so that it sticks to the card. Paint the pyramid sections.

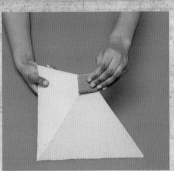

3 Leave the painted pyramid sections to dry in a warm place. When they are completely dry, sand down the tips until they are smooth and mask them off with tape.

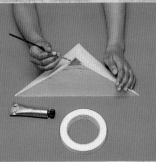

4 Now paint the tips of each half of the pyramid gold and leave to dry. Finally, glue the two halves together and place your pyramid on a bed of sand to display.

The building of the Great Pyramid probably took about 23 years. Originally the pyramids were cased in pale limestone, so they would have looked a brilliant white. The capstone at the very top of the pyramid was probably covered in gold.

The Valley of the Kings

I N 1550BC, the capital of Egypt moved south to Thebes. This marked the beginning of the New Kingdom. The ancient Egyptians no longer built pyramids as they were obvious targets for tomb robbers. The people still raised great temples to honour their dead rulers, but now the pharaohs were buried in secret underground tombs. These were hidden away in the cliffs bordering the desert on the west bank of the Nile, where the Sun set each night. It was from here that the pharaoh would journey to meet the Sun god on his death.

The burial sites near Thebes included the Valley of the Kings, the Valley of the Queens and the Valley of the Nobles. The tombs were packed with glittering treasure. Practical

items that the pharaoh would need in the next life were buried there too, such as food, royal clothing, gilded furniture, jewellery, weapons and chariots.

The tombs were guarded by a secret police force and were designed with traps to foil any intruders. Even so, many sites were robbed in ancient times. Luckily, some remained unspoiled and have given archaeologists an amazing look into the world of ancient Egypt.

THE KINGDOM OF THE DEAD
The Valley of the Kings lies across the Nile from the modern town of Luxor, on the edge of the Western desert. Sixty-two New Kingdom tombs have been discovered here so far.

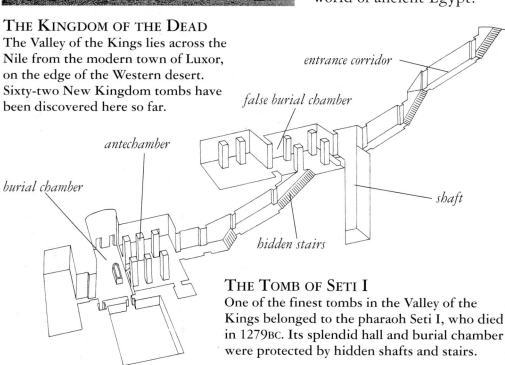

entrance corridor

false burial chamber

antechamber

burial chamber

shaft

hidden stairs

THE TOMB OF SETI I
One of the finest tombs in the Valley of the Kings belonged to the pharaoh Seti I, who died in 1279BC. Its splendid hall and burial chamber were protected by hidden shafts and stairs.

THE MASK
This beautiful mask was placed over the face of Tutankhamun's mummy. It presents the pharaoh in the image of the Sun god, Ra. This mask is made of solid gold and a blue stone called lapis lazuli. Tutankhamun's tomb was the most spectacular find in the Valley of the Kings. The inner chambers had not been disturbed for over 3,260 years.

GRAVE ROBBERS

When Howard Carter entered the tomb of Tutankhamun, he discovered that robbers had reached its outer chambers in ancient times. The Valley guards had resealed the tomb, but many items were left in heaps and piles. This picture shows two chariots, two beds, a chest, stools and food boxes.

UNTOLD TREASURES

This gold perfume box was found in Tutankhamun's burial chamber. The oval-shaped designs are called cartouches. They contain pictures of the pharaoh as a boy.

WORKERS ON SITE

The excavations of the 1800s and 1900s brought teams of Egyptian workers back into the Valley of the Kings for the first time in thousands of years. They dug down into tombs, carried out soil in baskets and shifted rocks. This photograph was taken in 1922 during Howard Carter's excavations that uncovered the tomb of Tutankhamun.

Mummies and Coffins

THE EARLY EGYPTIANS found out that people buried in the desert were often preserved in the dry sand. Their bodies dried out and became mummified. Over the ages, the Egyptians became experts at preserving bodies by embalming them. They believed that the dead would need to use their bodies in the next life.

The methods of mummification varied over the years. The process usually took about 70 days. The brains were hooked out through the nose and the other organs were removed and placed in special jars. Only the heart was left so that it could be weighed in the next life. Embalming involved drying the body out with salty crystals of natron. Afterwards it was stuffed and covered with oils and ointments and then wrapped in bandages. The mummy was then placed inside a series of coffins in the shape of the body.

MUMMY CASE

This beautiful gold case contains the mummy of a priestess. Once the embalmed body had been wrapped in bandages it was placed in a richly decorated coffin. Both the inside and outside would be covered in spells to help the dead person in the underworld. Sometimes more than one coffin was used. The inner coffins would be of brightly painted or gilded wood (*as left*) and the outer coffin would be a stone sarcophagus.

CANOPIC JARS

Special jars were used to store the body's organs. The human-headed jar held the liver. The baboon jar contained the lungs. The stomach was put in the jackal-headed jar and finally the guts were placed in the falcon-headed jar.

CANOPIC JARS

You will need: self-drying clay, rolling pin and board, ruler, modelling tool, sandpaper, masking tape, acrylic paint (white, blue, green, yellow, black), water pot and brush.

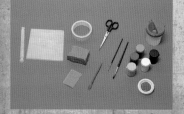

1 Roll out ³/₄ of the clay and cut out a circle about 7cm in diameter. This is the base of the jar. Now roll out thin strips of clay. Coil these from the base to make the sides.

2 Carefully press out the bumps between the coils until the sides of the jar are smooth and round. Finally trim the top of the jar with a modelling tool.

3 Now make a lid for the jar. Measure the size needed and cut out a circle of the remaining clay. Mould it into a dome. Model the head of a baboon on to the lid.

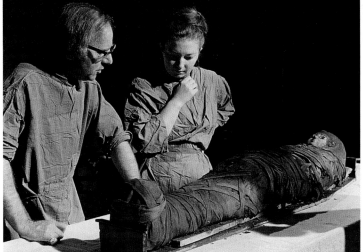

BENEATH THE BANDAGES

Unwrapping a mummy is a delicate operation. Today, archaeologists can use scanning or X-ray equipment to examine the mummies' bodies. It is possible to tell what food they once ate, the work they did and the illnesses they suffered from. X-rays also show the stuffing used to replace the internal organs.

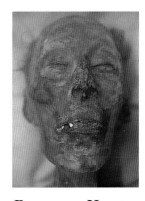

RAMESSES II

This is the unwrapped head of the mummy of Ramesses II. Wadding was placed in his eye sockets to stop the natron (preserving salts) from destroying his features.

THE OPENING OF THE MOUTH CEREMONY

The last ritual before burial was led by a priest wearing the mask of the god Anubis. The human-shaped coffin was held upright and its face was touched with magical instruments. This ceremony enabled the mummy to speak, see and hear in the next world.

It was believed that any part of a person's body could be used against them. For this reason the organs were removed and stored in canopic jars. Spells written on the jars protected them.

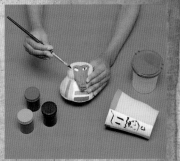

4 Hapy the baboon guarded the mummy's lungs. Use the modelling tool to make the baboon's eyes and long nose. Leave the lid in a warm place to dry.

5 When both the jar and the lid are completely dry, rub them down with sandpaper until they are smooth. The lid should fit snugly on to the jar.

6 It is now time to paint your jar. Use the masking tape to protect the baboon's face and to help you get the stripes straight. Follow the colours in the picture above.

7 Paint hieroglyphs down the front of the jar as shown. Use the letters on page 50–51 to help you. The canopic jar is now ready for the funeral.

Egyptian Funerals

WHEN A PHARAOH died, everything possible was done to make sure he completed his journey to the gods in safety. During the New Kingdom, the ruler's coffin, containing his mummy, would be placed on a boat and ferried from Thebes to the west bank of the Nile. There it was placed in a shrine and hauled on a sled drawn by oxen to the Valley of the Kings. The funeral procession was spectacular.

Priests scattered offerings of milk and burned incense. Women played the part of official mourners, screaming and weeping. In front of the tomb there was dancing and a priest read out spells. After a ceremony and a banquet, the coffin was placed in the tomb with food, drink and treasure. The tomb was then sealed.

LIFE AFTER DEATH
The *ba*, or personality, of a dead person hovers over the mummy. It appears as a bird. Its job is to help the dead body rejoin its spirit, or *ka*, so it can live in the next world. This picture is taken from a papyrus called the Book of the Dead. This book acted as a guide to the after-life for the dead. It contained spells to guarantee safe passage through the underworld. Priests read from it at the funeral and then it was buried with the mummy.

SHABTI FIGURES
Shabti were model figures placed in a tomb. Their purpose was to work for the dead person in the next life, acting as servants or labourers. They would be brought to life by a spell.

MAKE AN UDJAT EYE
You will need: self-drying clay, modelling tool, sandpaper, acrylic paint (red, blue, black, white), water pot and brush. Optional: rolling pin & board.

1 Begin by rolling out the clay on the board. Use the modelling tool to cut in the pattern of the eye pieces. Refer to step 2 for the shape of each piece.

2 Remove all extra clay and arrange the eye pieces on the board. The eye is meant to represent the eye of the falcon-headed god Horus.

3 Next, press the pieces together until you have the full shape of the eye. Use the modelling tool if necessary. Now leave the eye to dry.

THE FUNERAL PROCESSION

The coffin lies inside a boat-shaped shrine on a sled. The priests chant and pray as they begin to haul the sled up towards the burial place. A burial site such as the Valley of the Kings is called a necropolis, which means 'the city of the dead'. The coffin would be taken into the tomb through a deep corridor to its final resting place. In the burial chamber, it would be surrounded by fine objects and riches.

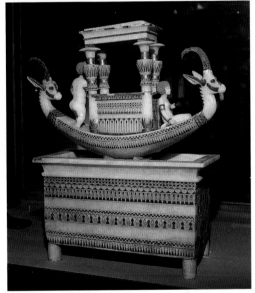

FUNERARY BOAT

This beautiful model boat was placed in the tomb of Tutankhamun. It is made of alabaster and shows two female mourners who represent the goddess Isis and her sister Nephthys. They are mourning the death of the murdered god Osiris. Between them is an empty sarcophagus (stone coffin casing), which may once have been used to hold oils. Many other boats were found in the tomb. They were meant to carry the pharaoh after he had died, just as a boat had carried Ra, the Sun god, through *Dwat*, the underworld.

4 Smooth the surface with fine sandpaper. The eye of Horus is now ready for painting. Horus was said to have lost his eye in a battle with Seth, the god of Chaos.

5 Paint in the white of the eye and add the black eyebrow and pupil. Next, paint in the red liner. Finally, paint the rest of the eye charm blue and leave to dry.

When Horus lost his eye, it was made better by the goddess Hathor. Udjat meant making better. Charms like this were wrapped up with mummies to protect them in the next life.

Priests, Temples and Festivals

MASSIVE TEMPLES were built in honour of the Egyptian gods. Many can still be seen today. They have great pillars and massive gates, courtyards and avenues of statues. Once, these would have led to a shrine that was believed to be the home of a god.

Ordinary people did not gather to worship in an Egyptian temple as they might today in a church. Only priests were allowed in the temples. They carried out rituals on behalf of the pharaoh, making offerings of food, burning incense, playing music and singing. They had complicated rules about washing and shaving their heads, and some had to wear special clothes such as leopard skins. Noblewomen served as priestesses during some ceremonies. Many priests had little knowledge of religion and just served in the temple for three months before returning to their normal work. Other priests studied the stars and spells.

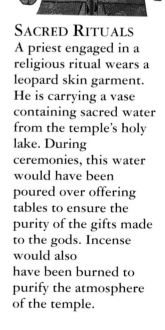

There were many religious festivals during which the god's shrine would be carried to other temples in a great procession. This was when ordinary Egyptians joined in worship. Offerings of food made to the gods were given back to the people for public feasting.

SACRED RITUALS
A priest engaged in a religious ritual wears a leopard skin garment. He is carrying a vase containing sacred water from the temple's holy lake. During ceremonies, this water would have been poured over offering tables to ensure the purity of the gifts made to the gods. Incense would also have been burned to purify the atmosphere of the temple.

KARNAK
This painting by David Roberts shows the massive temple of Karnak as it appeared in 1850. It still stands just outside the modern town of Luxor. The temple's most important god was Amun-Ra. The site also includes courts and buildings sacred to other gods and goddesses, including Mut (a vulture goddess, wife of Amun) and Khons (the Moon god, son of Amun). The Great Temple was enlarged and rebuilt over about 2,000 years.

TEMPLE OF HORUS
A statue of Horus, the falcon god, guards the temple at Edfu. There was a temple on this site during the New Kingdom. However, the building that still stands today dates back to the period of Greek rule. This temple was dedicated to Horus and his wife, the cow goddess Hathor. Inside the temple there are stone carvings showing Horus fighting the enemies of Osiris, his father.

ANUBIS THE EMBALMER
A priest wears the mask of Anubis to embalm a body. This jackal-headed god was said to have prepared the body of the god Osiris for burial. He and his priests had strong links with mummies and the practice of embalming.

KALABSHA TEMPLE
The Kalabsha temple was one of the largest temples in Lower Nubia. In the 1960s, the Aswan Dam was built and Lower Nubia was flooded. Many monuments such as the temples at Abu Simbel and Philae had to be moved. The temple at Kalabsha was dismantled, and its 13,000 blocks of stone were moved to New Kalabsha, where it was rebuilt.

GATEWAY TO ISIS
The temple of Philae (*above*) was built in honour of Isis, the mother goddess. Isis was worshipped all over Egypt and in many other lands, too. Massive gateways called pylons guard the temple of Philae. Pylons guard the way to many Egyptian temples and were used for special ceremonies.

Workers and Slaves

THE PHARAOHS may have believed that it was their links with the gods that kept Egypt going, but really it was the hard work of the ordinary people. It was they who dug the soil, worked in the mines and quarries, sailed the boats on the river Nile, marched with the army into Syria or Nubia, cooked food and raised children.

Slavery was not very important in ancient Egypt, but it did exist. Most of the slaves were prisoners who had been captured during the many wars that Egypt fought with their neighbours in the Near East. Slaves were usually treated well and were allowed to own property.

Many Egyptian workers were serfs. This meant that their freedom was limited. They could be bought and sold along with the estates where they worked. Farmers had to be registered with the government. They had to sell crops at a fixed price and pay taxes in the form of produce. During the season of the Nile floods, when the fields lay under water, many workers were recruited into public building projects. Punishment for those who ran away was harsh.

PLOUGHING WITH OXEN
This model figure from a tomb is ploughing the soil with oxen. The Egyptian farm workers' daily toil was hard. Unskilled peasant labourers did not own land and were paid little.

TRANSPORTING A STATUE
These workers are moving a huge stone statue on a wooden sled hauled by ropes. Many farm workers had to labour on large public building works, building dams or pyramids, each summer and autumn. Their food and lodging were provided, but they were not paid wages. Only the official classes were exempt from this service, but anyone rich enough could pay someone else to do the work for them. Slaves were used for really hard labour, such as mining and quarrying.

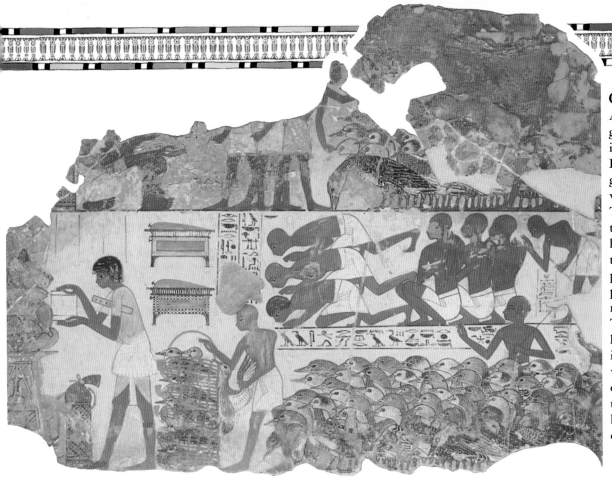

COUNTING GEESE

A farmer's flock of geese is counted out in this wall painting. Every other year, government officials visited each farm. They would count the animals to see how much tax had to be paid to the pharaoh. Taxes were paid in produce rather than money. The scribe on the left is recording this information. Scribes were members of the official classes and therefore had a higher position than other workers.

GIVE THAT MAN A BEATING

This tomb painting shows an official overseeing work in the fields. Unskilled peasant farmers were attached to an estate belonging to the pharaoh, a temple, or a rich landowner. Farmers who could not or would not give a large percentage of their harvest in rent and taxes to the pharaoh were punished harshly. They might be beaten, and their tools or their house could be seized as payment. There were law courts, judges and local magistrates in place to punish tax collectors who took bribes.

CARRYING BREAD

A woman carries a tray of loaves on her head. Most of the cooking in large houses and palaces was done by male servants, but baking bread was the job of the women. Baking was one of the few public jobs open to women.

GRINDING CORN

This model from 2325BC shows a female servant grinding wheat or barley grains into flour. She is using a stone hand-mill called a quern.

Farmers and Crops

THE ANCIENT EGYPTIANS called the banks of the Nile the Black Land because of the mud that was washed downstream each year from Central Africa. The Nile flooded in June, depositing this rich, fertile mud in Egypt. The land remained underwater until autumn.

By November the ground was ready for ploughing and then sowing. Seeds were scattered over the soil and trampled in by the hooves of sheep or goats. During the drier periods of the year, farmers dug channels and canals to bring water to irrigate their land. In the New Kingdom, a lifting system called the *shaduf* was introduced to raise water from the river. The success of this farming cycle was vital. Years of low flood or drought could spell disaster. If the crops failed, people went hungry.

HARVEST FESTIVAL
A priestess makes an offering of harvest produce in the tomb of Nakht. The picture shows some of the delicious fruits grown in Egypt. These included figs, grapes and pomegranates.

FARMING TOOLS
Hoes were used to break up soil that had been too heavy for the ploughs. They were also used for digging soil. The sharp sickle was used to cut grain.

Farm animals included ducks, geese, pigs, sheep and goats. Cows grazed the fringes of the desert or the greener lands of the delta region. Oxen were used for hauling ploughs and donkeys were widely used to carry goods.

sickle   *hoes*

TOILING IN THE FIELDS
Grain crops were usually harvested in March or April, before the great heat began. The ears of wheat or barley were cut off with a sickle made of wood and sharpened flint. In some well-irrigated areas there was a second harvest later in the summer.

MAKE A SHADUF
You will need: card, pencil, ruler, scissors, pva glue, masking tape, acrylic paint (blue, green, brown), water pot and brush, balsa wood strips, small stones, twig, clay, hessian, string. Note: mix green paint with dried herbs for the grass mixture.

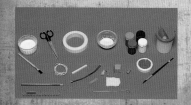

c = water tank

15cm
5cm
5cm
2.5 cm
3cm
2.5 cm
9cm
9cm
9cm
23cm
23cm
a
23cm
c
3.5cm
2.5 cm
3.5 cm
16cm
7cm
4cm
5cm
5cm
b
23cm
23cm
23cm
15cm
8cm
4cm
3.5cm
7cm
b = river

a = irrigation channel & river bank

Cut out the cardboard shapes (a), (b) and (c) as shown.

1 Glue the edges of boxes (a), (b) and (c), as shown. Bind them with masking tape until they are dry. Paint the river (b) and the water tank (c) blue and leave to dry.

HERDING THE OXEN

This New Kingdom wall painting shows oxen being herded in front of a government inspector. Cattle were already being bred along the banks of the Nile in the days before the pharaohs. They provided milk, meat and leather. They hauled wooden ploughs and were killed as sacrifices to the gods in the temples.

NILE CROPS

The chief crops were barley and wheat, used for making beer and bread. Beans and lentils were grown alongside leeks, onions, cabbages, radishes, lettuces and cucumbers. Juicy melons, dates and figs could be grown in desert oases. Grapes were grown in vineyards.

leeks   *onions*

WATERING MACHINE

The *shaduf* has a bucket on one end of a pole and a heavy weight at the other. First the weight is pushed up, lowering the bucket into the river. As the weight is lowered, it raises up the full bucket.

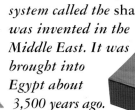

The mechanical lifting system called the shaduf *was invented in the Middle East. It was brought into Egypt about 3,500 years ago.*

2 Paint the river bank with the green grass mixture on top, brown on the sides and the irrigation channel blue. Next, get the balsa strips for the frame of the shaduf.

3 Glue the strips together, supporting them with masking tape and a piece of card. When dry, paint the frame brown. Glue the stones onto the water tank.

4 Use a twig for the shaduf pole. Make a weight from clay wrapped in hessian. Tie it to one end of the pole. Make a bucket from clay, leaving two holes for the string.

5 Thread the string through the bucket and tie to the pole. Tie the pole, with its weight and bucket, to the shaduf frame. Finally, glue the frame to the bank.

Food and Banquets

Working people in Egypt were often paid in food. They ate bread, onions and salted fish, washed down with a sweet, grainy beer. Flour was often gritty and the teeth of many mummies show signs of severe wear and tear. Dough was kneaded with the feet or by hand, and pastry cooks produced all kinds of cakes and loaves.

Beautiful Bowls
Dishes and bowls were often made of faience, a glassy pottery. The usual colour for this attractive tableware was blue-green or turquoise.

A big banquet for a pharaoh was a grand affair, with guests dressed in their finest clothes. A royal menu might include roast goose or stewed beef, kidneys, wild duck or tender gazelle. Lamb was not eaten for religious reasons, and in some regions certain types of fish were also forbidden. Vegetables such as leeks were stewed with milk and cheese. Egyptian cooks were experts at stewing, roasting and baking.

Red and white wines were served at banquets. They were stored in pottery jars marked with their year and their vineyard, just like the labels on modern wine bottles.

A Feast Fit for a King
New Kingdom noblewomen exchange gossip at a dinner party. They show off their jewellery and best clothes. The Egyptians loved wining and dining. They would be entertained by musicians, dancers and acrobats during the feast.

Make a Cake

You will need: 200g stoneground flour, $\frac{1}{2}$ tsp salt, 1tsp baking powder, 75g butter, 60g honey, 3tbsp milk, caraway seeds, bowl, wooden spoon, floured surface, baking tray.

1 Begin by mixing together the flour, salt and baking powder in the bowl. Next, chop up the butter and add it to the mixture.

2 Using your fingers, rub the butter into the mixture, as shown. Your mixture should look like fine breadcrumbs when you have finished.

3 Now add 40g of your honey. Combine it with your mixture. This will sweeten your cakes. The ancient Egyptians did not have sugar.

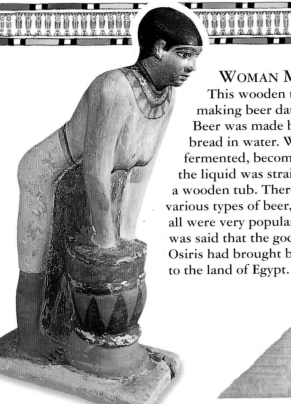

WOMAN MAKING BEER

This wooden tomb model of a woman making beer dates back to 2400BC. Beer was made by mashing barley bread in water. When the mixture fermented, becoming alcoholic, the liquid was strained off into a wooden tub. There were various types of beer, but all were very popular. It was said that the god Osiris had brought beer to the land of Egypt.

DRINKING VESSEL

This beautiful faience cup could have been used to drink wine, water or beer. It is decorated with a pattern of lotus flowers.

DESERT DESSERTS

An Egyptian meal could be finished off with nuts such as almonds or sweet fruits – juicy figs, dates, grapes, pomegranates or melons. Sugar was still unknown so honey was used to sweeten cakes and pastries.

pomegranates

dates

PALACE BAKERY

Whole teams of model cooks and bakers were left in some tombs. This was so that a pharaoh could order them to put on a good banquet to entertain his guests in the other world. Models are shown sifting, mixing and kneading flour, and making pastries. Most of our knowledge about Egyptian food and cooking comes from the food boxes and offerings left in tombs.

Egyptian pastries were often shaped in spirals like these. Other popular shapes were rings like doughnuts, and pyramids. Some were shaped like crocodiles!

4 Add the milk and stir the mixture until it forms a dough. Make your dough into a ball and place it on a floured board or surface. Divide the dough into three.

5 Roll the dough into long strips, as shown. Take the strips and coil them into a spiral to make one cake. Make the other cakes in the same way.

6 Now sprinkle each cake with caraway seeds and place them on a greased baking tray. Finish off by glazing the cakes carefully with a little extra honey.

7 Ask an adult to bake them in an oven at 180°C/Gas Mark 4 for 20 minutes. When they are ready, take them out and leave on a baking rack to cool.

Egyptian Dress

THE MOST COMMON TEXTILE in Egypt was linen. It was mostly a spotless white. Dyes such as iron (red), indigo (blue) and saffron (yellow) were sometimes used, but coloured and patterned clothes were usually the mark of a foreigner. However, the Egyptians did decorate their clothes with beads and beautiful feathers. Wool was not used for weaving in ancient Egypt. Silk and cotton did not appear until foreign rulers came to power in Egypt, after about 1000BC.

The basic items of dress for men were a simple kilt, loin-cloth or tunic. Women wore a long, closely fitting dress of fine fabric. Fashions for both men and women varied over the ages, with changes in the straps, pleating and folds.

Although more elaborate styles of clothing did appear in the New Kingdom, clothing was relatively simple, with elaborate wigs, jewellery and eye make-up creating a more dramatic effect.

LUCKY BRACELET
The bracelet above features an *udjat* eye – this eye charm was thought to protect those who carried it. Many items of jewellery featured such charms for decoration as well as for superstitious reasons. Some necklaces and earrings featured magic charms to prevent snake bites or other disasters.

GOLDEN SANDALS
These gold sandals were found in the tomb of Sheshonq II. Sandals for the rich were usually made of fine leather, while the poor used sandals made of papyrus or woven grass.

FABRICS

Linen was made from the plant flax. Its stalks were soaked, pounded and then rolled into lengths. The fibre was spun into thread by hand on a whirling spindle, and the thread kept moist in the mouths of the spinners. It was then ready for weaving. The first Egyptian looms were flat, but upright looms were brought in during the Hyksos period.

linen

FIT FOR A KING AND QUEEN

This panel from a golden throne shows Tutankhamun and his wife, Ankhesenamun, in their palace. The pictures are made from glass, silver, precious stones and faience (glazed pottery). The queen is wearing a long, pleated dress, while the pharaoh wears a pleated kilt. Garments were draped around the wearer rather than sewn, and pleating was very popular from the Middle Kingdom onwards. Both Tutankhamun and his wife wear sandals, bracelets, wide collars and beautiful headdresses or crowns. The queen is offering her husband perfume or ointment from a bowl.

FIRST FASHIONS

This shirt was found in the tomb of Tarkhan. It was made nearly 5,000 years ago during the reign of the pharaoh Djet. The fabric is linen and there are pleats across the shoulders.

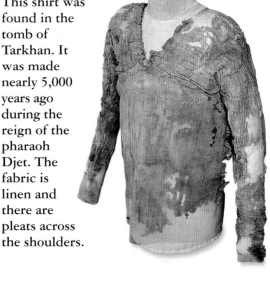

COLOURFUL COLLARS

Wide, brilliantly coloured collars were made of glass beads, flowers, berries and leaves. They were worn for banquets and other special occasions. Collars found in Tutankhamun's tomb included those made of olive leaves and cornflowers. By examining such plants, archaeologists can find out important information about gardening, farming, the climate and insect life in ancient Egypt.

Looking Beautiful

BOTH EGYPTIAN MEN and women wore cosmetics. Their make-up included green eyeshadow made from a mineral called malachite and black eyeliner made from galena, a type of lead. Lipsticks and blusher were made from red ochre, and the early Egyptians also liked tattoos. Most Egyptian men were clean shaven. Priests also shaved their heads and the short haircut of the pharaoh was always kept covered in public. Wigs were worn by men and women, even by those who had plenty of hair of their own. Grey hair was dyed and there were various remedies for baldness. One was a lotion made from donkey's hoof, dog's paw, date stones and oil!

A TIMELESS BEAUTY
This limestone head is of Queen Nefertiti, the wife of the Sun-worshipping pharaoh Akhenaten. She seems to be the ideal of Egyptian beauty. She wears a headdress and a necklace. The stone is painted and so we can see that she is also wearing make-up and lipstick.

MIRROR, MIRROR
Mirrors were made of polished copper or bronze, with handles of wood or ivory. This bronze mirror is from 1900BC. Mirrors were used by the wealthy for checking hairstyles, applying make-up, or simply for admiring one's own good looks! The poor had to make do with seeing their reflection in water.

MAKE A MIRROR

You will need: mirror card, pencil, scissors, self-drying clay, modelling tool, rolling pin and board, small piece of card or sandpaper, gold paint, pva glue and brush, waterpot and brush.

1 Begin by drawing a mirror shape on the white side of a piece of mirror card, as shown. Carefully cut the mirror shape out. Put the card to one side.

2 Take your clay and roll it into a tube. Then mould it into a handle shape, as shown. Decorate the handle with a lotus or papyrus flower, or other design.

3 Now make a slot in the handle with a square piece of card or sandpaper, as shown. This is where the mirror card will slot into the handle.

BIG WIGS AND WAXY CONES

Many pictures show nobles at banquets wearing cones of perfumed grease on their heads. The scent may have been released as the cones melted in the heat. However, some experts believe that the cones were drawn in by artists to show that the person was wearing a scented wig. False hairpieces and wigs were very popular in Egypt. It was common for people to cut their hair short, but some did have long hair that they dressed in elaborate styles.

COSMETICS

During the early years of the Egyptian Empire, black eye kohl was made from galena, a type of poisonous lead! Later soot was used. Henna was painted on the nails and the soles of the feet to make them red. Popular beauty treatments included pumice stone to smooth rough skin and ash face packs.

face pack   *pumice stone*   *kohl*   *henna*

COSMETICS BOWL

Cosmetics, oils and lotions were prepared and stored in jars and bowls, as well as in hollow reeds or tubes. These containers were made of stone, pottery and glass. Minerals were ground into a powder and then mixed with water in cosmetics bowls to make a paste. Make-up was applied with the fingers or with a special wooden applicator. Two colours of eye make-up were commonly used – green and black. Green was used in the early period, but later the distinctive black eye paint became more popular.

The shape of mirrors and their shining surface reminded Egyptians of the Sun disc, so they became religious symbols. By the New Kingdom, many were decorated with the goddess Hathor or lotus flowers.

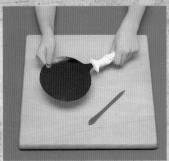

4 Place the handle on a wire baking tray, and leave it in a warm place to dry. Turn it over after two hours. When it is completely dry, try your mirror for size.

5 It is now time to paint the handle. Paint one side carefully with gold paint and leave it to dry. When it has dried, turn the handle over and paint the other side.

6 Finally, you can assemble your mirror. Cover the base of the mirror card in glue and insert it into the handle slot. Leave it in a warm place to dry.

Papyrus and Scribes

THE WORD PAPER comes from papyrus, the reed that grows on the banks of the river Nile. To make paper, the Egyptians peeled the outer layer off the reeds. The pith inside the stems was cut into strips, soaked in water and then placed in criss-cross layers. These were hammered until they were squashed together. The surface of the papyrus was then smoothed out with a wooden tool. Other writing materials included fragments of pottery, leather and plastered boards.

It is thought that only about four out of every 1,000 Egyptians could read or write. Scribes were professional writers who would copy out official records and documents, letters, poems and stories. The training of young scribes was thorough, strict and harsh. One teacher, Amenemope, wrote to his students, "pass no day in idleness or you will be beaten". However, most workers envied the scribes for their easy way of life. They were well rewarded for their work.

SCRIBE'S BURNISHER
This beautiful tool was found in the tomb of Tutankhamun. It is made of ivory topped with gold foil. Burnishers were used for smoothing down the surface of freshly-made papyrus.

EXERCISE BOOKS
School exercises were often written on broken pieces of stone or pottery that had been thrown away. These pieces are known as *ostraka*. Young scribes would copy exercises out onto the ostrakon and then have them corrected by a teacher. Many examples of corrected exercises have been discovered in Egypt.

SCRIBES RECORDING THE HARVEST
Kneeling scribes record the size of the grain harvest. The farmer would then have to give a proportion of the grain to the pharaoh as a tax. Many scribes worked in the government, copying out accounts, taxes, orders and laws. They were like civil servants.

WRITING CASE

This scribe's pen-case dates back to around 3000BC. It contains reed pens and an inkwell. The ink was made of charcoal or soot, mixed with water. Scribes carried a grinder for crushing the pigments first. Often the scribe's name and the name of his employer or the pharaoh would be carved into the case.

PENS

In ancient Egypt brushes and pens were made of reed. Blocks of ink were mixed with water on a special palette. Black ink was made from charcoal and red ink was made from ochre (an iron compound). Both were mixed with gum.

charcoal

reed pen

PORTABLE PALETTE

The work of a scribe often meant he had to travel on business, to record official documents. Most had a portable palette like this for when they went away. Scribes often carried a briefcase or document carrier too, to protect the information they had recorded.

SYMBOL FOR A SCRIBE

The hieroglyph for a scribe is made up of a water pot, a brush holder and a palette with cakes of ink. The Egyptian word for scribe or official was *sesh*.

FAMOUS SCRIBES

Accroupi sits cross-legged, holding a scroll of papyrus and a pen-case. Accroupi was a famous scribe who lived in Egypt at the time of the Old Kingdom. Scribes were often powerful people in ancient Egypt, and many statues of them have survived. The high standing of scribes is confirmed in the text *Satire of the Trades,* which says: "Behold! no scribe is short of food and of riches from the palace".

Ways of Writing

WE KNOW so much about the ancient Egyptians because of the written language they left behind. Inscriptions providing detailed information about their lives can be found on everything from obelisks to tombs. From about 3100BC they used pictures called hieroglyphs. Each of these could stand for an object, an idea or a sound. There were originally around 1,000 hieroglyphic symbols. Hieroglyphs were used for thousands of years, but from 1780BC a script called hieratic was also popular. Yet another script, demotic, was used as well as hieroglyphs in the latter days of ancient Egypt.

However, by AD600, long after the last of the pharaohs, no one understood hieroglyphs. The secrets of ancient Egypt were lost for 1,200 years, until the discovery of the Rosetta Stone.

THE ROSETTA STONE
The discovery of the Rosetta Stone was a lucky accident. In 1799, a French soldier discovered a piece of stone at an Egyptian village called el-Rashid or Rosetta. On the stone, the same words were written in three scripts representing two languages. Hieroglyphic text is at the top, demotic text is in the centre, and Greek is at the bottom.

EGYPTIAN CODE CRACKED
French scholar Jean-François Champollion cracked the Rosetta Stone code in 1822. The stone contains a royal decree written in 196BC when the Greek king Ptolemy V was in power in Egypt. The Greek on the stone enabled Champollion to translate the hieroglyphs. This one discovery is central to our understanding of the way the ancient Egyptians used to live.

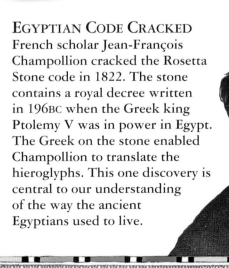

A

M

Motion

OU

W

N

Overseas

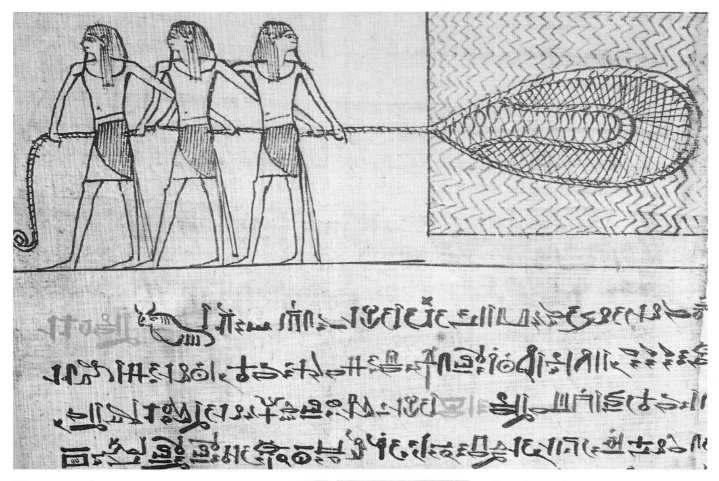

HIERATIC SCRIPT
Hieratic script (*above*) took the picture symbols of hieroglyphs and turned them into shapes that were more like letters. This script was more flowing and could be written quickly. It was used for stories, letters and business contracts. It was always read from right to left.

DEMOTIC SCRIPT
Demotic script (*left*) was introduced towards the end of the Late Kingdom. This could be written even more quickly than hieratic script. Initially it was used for business, but soon it was also being used for religious and scientific writings. It disappeared when Egypt came under Roman rule.

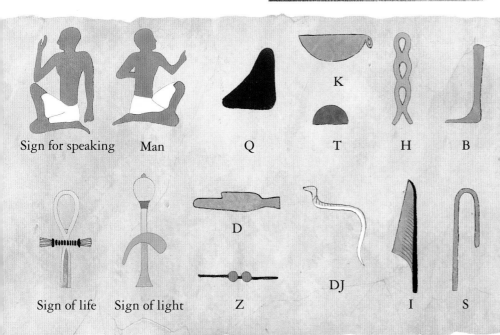

Sign for speaking   Man   Q   K   T   H   B

D

Sign of life   Sign of light   Z   DJ   I   S

HIEROGLYPHS
Hieroglyphs were made up of small pictures. These pictures were based on simplified sketches of birds and snakes, plants, parts of the body, boats and houses. Some hieroglyphs represented complete ideas such as light, travel or life. Others stood for letters or sounds that could be combined to make words.

Science and Technology

THE ANCIENT EGYPTIANS had advanced systems of numbering and measuring. They put their knowledge to good use in building, engineering and in surveying land. However, their knowledge of science was often mixed up with superstitions and belief in magic. For example, doctors understood a lot about broken bones and surgery, but at the same time they used all kinds of spells, amulets and magic potions to ward off disease. Much of their knowledge about the human body came from their experience of preparing the dead for burial.

The priests studied the stars carefully. They thought that the planets must be gods. The Egyptians also worked out a calendar, and this was very important for deciding when the Nile floods would arrive and when to plant crops.

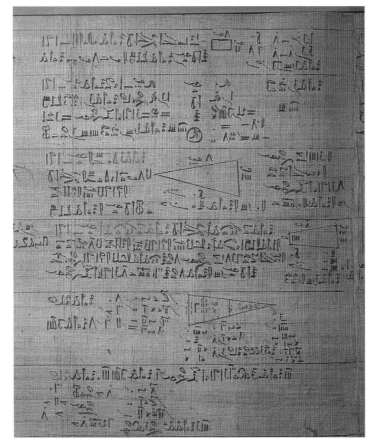

MATHEMATICAL PAPYRUS
This papyrus shows methods for working out the areas of squares, circles and triangles. It dates from around 850BC. These methods would have been used in calculations for land areas and pyramid heights on Egyptian building projects. Other surviving Egyptian writings show mathematical calculations to work out how much grain would fit into a store. The Egyptians used a decimal system of numbering with separate symbols for one, ten, 100 and 1,000. Eight was shown by eight one symbols – 11111111.

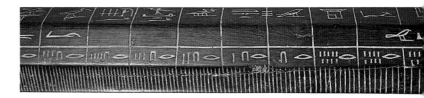

CUBIT MEASURE
Units of measurement included the royal cubit of about 52cm and the short cubit of 45cm. A cubit was the length of a man's forearm and was subdivided into palms and fingers.

MAKE A WATER CLOCK
You will need: self-drying clay, plastic flowerpot, modelling tool, skewer, pencil, ruler, masking tape, scissors, yellow acrylic paint, varnish, water pot and brush. Optional: rolling pin and board.

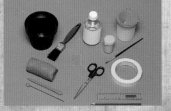

1 Begin by rolling out the clay. Take the plastic flowerpot and press its base firmly into the clay. This will be the bottom of your water clock.

2 Cut out an oblong of clay large enough to mould around the flowerpot. Add the base and use your modelling tool to make the joints smooth.

3 Make a small hole near the bottom of the pot with a skewer, as shown. Leave the pot in a warm place to dry. When the clay has dried, remove the flowerpot.

NILOMETER

A series of steps called a Nilometer was used to measure the depth of the water in the river Nile. The annual floods were desperately important for the farmers living alongside the Nile.

A good flood measured about 7m. More than this and farm buildings and channels might be destroyed. Less than this and the fields might go dry.

MEDICINE

Most Egyptian medicines were based on plants. One cure for headaches included juniper berries, coriander, wormwood and honey. The mixture was rubbed into the scalp. Other remedies included natron (a kind of salt), myrrh and even crocodile droppings. Some Egyptian medicines probably did heal the patients, but others did more harm than good.

coriander

garlic

STAR OF THE NILE

This astronomical painting is from the ceiling of the tomb of Seti I. The study of the stars was part religion, part science. The brightest star in the sky was Sirius, which we call the dog star. The Egyptians called it Sopdet, after a goddess. This star rose into view at the time when the Nile floods were due and was greeted with a special festival.

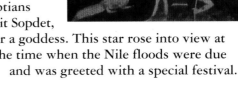

Time was calculated on water clocks by calculating how long it took for water to drop from level to level. The water level lowered as it dripped through the hole in the bottom of the pot.

4 Mark out lines at 3mm intervals inside the pot. Mask the ends with tape and paint the lines yellow. When dry, remove the tape. Ask an adult to varnish the pot inside.

5 Find or make another two pots and position them as shown. Ask a partner to put their finger over the hole in the clock while you pour water into it.

6 Now ask your partner to take their finger away. The length of time it takes for the level of the water to drop from mark to mark is the measure of time.

Music and Dance

ALTHOUGH MUCH OF OUR KNOWLEDGE about the Egyptians comes from their interest in death, they also loved life. Paintings show how much they enjoyed dancing and music. Also, many musical instruments have been found inside tombs. Music was played for pleasure and entertainment, as well as for religious worship and for marching into battle.

The first Egyptian instruments were probably flutes and harps. Instruments similar to pipes, oboes and trumpets later became popular. During the New Kingdom, lutes and lyres were brought in from Asia. Bells, cymbals, tambourines and drums kept the beat, along with a sacred rattle called the sistrum.

Dancers performed at banquets, sometimes doing acrobatic feats in time to the music. Other dances were more solemn, being performed in temples and at funerals.

THE SISTRUM
A priestess is rattling a sistrum. The ancient Egyptians called this instrument a *seshesht*. It is made of a loop of bronze containing loose rods that rattled when shaken.

STRING SOUNDS
Musicians play a harp, a lyre and a lute at a banquet. These were among the most common string instruments in ancient Egypt. During the New Kingdom female musicians became very popular.

MAKE A RATTLE

You will need: self-drying clay, balsa wood (1.5 x 15cm), card, modelling tool, skewer, wire and 10 washers, pliers, pva glue and brush, acrylic paint (brown or red and black mixed, gold), water pot and brush.

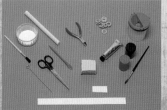

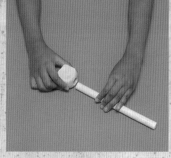

1 For the handle, you will need the block of clay and the balsa wood. Push the balsa wood into the square block of clay to make a hole for the handle.

2 Next, make two slots in the top of the clay block for the card part of the rattle to fit into. The card will form the shaker part of the sistrum.

3 Sculpt the face of the goddess Hathor into the top of the handle. Look at the picture of her on page 18. Now leave the clay in a warm place to dry.

MUSICIANS OF THEBES

This famous wall painting from Thebes is about 3,400 years old. It shows women dancers and musicians performing at a banquet. The Egyptians tended to listen to professional musicians rather than play for their own pleasure. No Egyptian music was written down, but we do still know the words of some of their songs. The hieroglyphs above this picture tell us that the musicians are playing a song in praise of nature. The dancing girls in the painting shake their bodies gracefully to the rhythm of the music.

HARPIST

A male harpist plays a hymn to the god Horus. The first Egyptian harps were plain and simple, but later they were beautifully made, carved and painted gold.

4 Pierce two holes into the card. Thread the wire through the washers and then through the holes in the card. Bend the wire back with pliers to secure it.

5 Push the head of the rattle into the slots in the handle and then glue into position. Paint the rattle brown and rub in gold paint to create a bronze look.

The sistrum was a sacred rattle used by noblewomen and priestesses at religious ceremonies and musical festivities. It was used in the worship of Hathor, the goddess of love.

Entertainment and Leisure

ONE OF THE FAVOURITE PASTIMES of the Egyptians was hunting. They hunted for pleasure as well as for food, using bows and arrows, throwing sticks, spears and nets. Thousands of years ago, many wild animals lived in Egypt. Today most of these are found only in lands far to the south. They included hippopotamuses and lions. Hunting these animals was extremely dangerous, and pictures show the pharaoh setting out bravely for the hunt. In practice the animals were often trapped and released into an enclosure before the pharaoh arrived. There he could easily catch them from the safety of his chariot.

ANIMAL CHAMPIONS
Here the lion and the antelope, two old enemies, are sitting down peacefully for a game of *senet*. This painting dates from about 1150BC. *Senet* could be played on fine boards or on simple grids scratched on stones or drawn in sand.

Chariots first appeared in Egypt during the Hyksos period, and racing them soon became a fashionable sport with the nobles. One sport that was popular with all Egyptians was wrestling. There was no theatre in Egypt, but storytellers at the royal court and on village streets told fables and stories about battles, gods and magic.

Board games were popular from the early days of Egypt. In the tomb of Tutankhamun there was a beautiful gaming board made of ebony and ivory, designed for two games called *senet* and *tjau*.

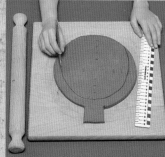

YOUR MOVE
This noble is playing *senet*, eagerly watched by his wife. The players threw dice to decide how many squares to move over at one time. Some of the squares had forfeits and some had gains. *Senet* was said to be a game of struggle against evil.

MAKE A MEHEN BOARD
You will need: self-drying clay, rolling pin and board, ruler, modelling tool, green paint, cloth, varnish, water pot and brush.
For the game: 12 round counters 6 blue on one side/grey on the other, 6 gold on one side/orange on the other, 2 larger counters, dice.

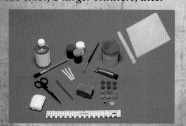

1 Roll out the clay onto the board and cut it to the shape shown. Use the ruler and modelling tool to score on the lines of the snake at regular intervals. Leave to dry.

2 Next, rub the board with diluted green paint to stain the lines. Wipe the excess paint away with a rag. Leave it to dry. Finally, ask an adult to varnish it.

3 Each player has 6 counters of the same colours plus a larger piece (the lion). Turn all your counters so they show the same colour. You need to throw a one to start each counter off.

THE LAST GAME

This gaming board comes from Tutankhamun's tomb. Board games were so popular that they were placed in tombs to offer the dead person some fun in the next life.

HOLDS AND THROWS

Wrestling was one sport that any Egyptian could do. It did not need expensive chariots or any other special equipment. It was popular with rich and poor alike.

WILDFOWLING IN THE MARSHES

Nebamun, a nobleman, is enjoying a day's wildfowling in the marshes of the Nile Delta. He stands in his reed boat and hurls a throwing stick, a kind of boomerang, at the birds flying out of the reeds. His cat already seems to have caught several birds.

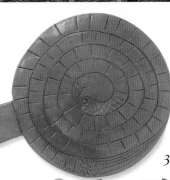

Mehen, the snake game, was popular in Egypt before 3000BC.

4 You must start each of your counters on the board before advancing any of the others. A throw of one ends a go and allows your opponent to take their turn.

5 Exact numbers are needed to reach the centre. Once at the centre, turn your counter over to start its return journey. When it has got back to the start, your lion piece can begin.

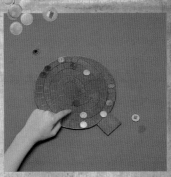

6 The lion moves to the centre in the same way as the other counters. However, on its return journey, it can eat any of your opponent's counters in its way.

7 The winner is the person whose lion has eaten the largest number of counters. Work out the number of counters you got home safely and see who has the most left.

A Child's World

ALTHOUGH EGYPTIAN CHILDREN had only a brief period of childhood before education and work, they did enjoy playing with rattles, balls, spinning tops, toy horses and toy crocodiles. They wrestled in the dust, ran races and swam in the river.

Girls from ordinary Egyptian families received little schooling. They were taught how to look after the household, how to spin, weave and cook. When girls grew up there were few jobs open to them, although they did have legal rights and some noblewomen became very powerful. Boys were mostly trained to do the same jobs as their fathers. Some went to scribe school, where they learned how to read and write. Slow learners were beaten without mercy. Boys and some girls from noble families received a broader education, learning how to read, write and do sums.

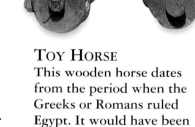

TOY HORSE
This wooden horse dates from the period when the Greeks or Romans ruled Egypt. It would have been pulled along on its wheels by a piece of string.

FUN FOR ALL
Spinning tops were popular toys with children in Egypt. They were made of glazed stone and would have been cheap enough for poorer families to buy.

ISIS AND HORUS
Many statues show the goddess Isis with Horus as a child sitting on his mother's lap. The young Horus was believed to protect families from danger and accidents. The Egyptians had large families and family life was important to them.

A LION THAT ROARS
You will need: self-drying clay, rolling pin and board, modelling tool, a piece of card, skewer, balsa wood, sandpaper, acrylic paint (white, green, red, blue, black, yellow), masking tape, string, water pot & brush.

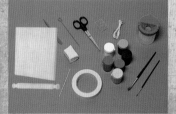

1 Begin by rolling out the clay. Cut the pieces to the shapes shown. Mould the legs onto the body and the base. Put the bottom jaw piece to one side.

2 Use your modelling tool to make a hole between the lion's upper body and the base, as shown. This hole is for the lower jaw to fit into.

3 Insert the lower jaw into the hole you have just made and prop it up with a piece of card. Make a hole through the upper and lower jaws with the skewer.

THE LOCK OF YOUTH

When they were young, boys and girls wore a special haircut, a shaved head with a lock of plaited hair. This plait, or lock of youth, was allowed to grow over one side of children's faces. When they reached adulthood, many Egyptians would have their heads shaved and wear an elaborate wig.

Originally this toy would have been made of wood, with a bronze tooth.

BOUNCING BACK

Egyptian children enjoyed playing games with balls made from rags, linen and reeds. However, archaeologists are not certain whether the balls above were used for the playing of games or as a type of rattle for younger children.

A TOY LION

Pull the string, and the lion roars! Or is it a cat miaowing? Children once played with this animal on the banks of the Nile. At the time, this toy would have been brightly painted.

4 Now use the skewer to make a hole from left to right through the lion's upper body. The string will go through these holes later to be connected to the jaw.

5 Push a small piece of balsa wood into the mouth. This will form the lion's tooth. Leave the clay lion to dry and then sand down the surface.

6 Paint the lion in white, yellow, blue, black and red, as shown. Use masking tape to ensure that your lines are straight. Leave the lion in a warm place to dry.

7 Thread the string through the holes in the upper body and tie it to secure. A second string then goes through the lower and upper jaws of your lion.

Weapons and Warriors

EGYPT was surrounded by harsh deserts on three sides. In the north were the marshes of the delta and to the south the Nile ran over a series of rapids and waterfalls, the cataracts. All these formed barriers to invading armies. Even so, Egyptian towns were defended with forts and walls, and many pharaohs went into battle against their neighbours. Wars were fought against the Libyans, the Nubians, the Hittites and the Syrians.

There were professional soldiers in Egypt, but most were forced to join the army. For slaves, fighting in the army was a chance to gain their freedom. At times, foreign troops were also hired to fight. Young men in the villages learned to drill in preparation for war. Soldiers carried shields of leather and wood. They were armed with spears, axes, bows and arrows, daggers and swords. Later, war chariots drawn by horses were used. Special awards, such as the golden fly, were handed out for bravery in battle.

KING DEN
This ivory label from 3000BC shows King Den striding into battle against an eastern enemy. He stands beneath the flag, or standard, of the jackal-headed god Anubis. He is armed with a club, or mace.

RIDING TO VICTORY
Egyptian art often shows scenes of a pharaoh riding into battle or returning home in triumph. The king is shown in a fine chariot, driving prisoners before him. Artists often showed the enemy as very small, to show the importance and power of the pharaoh. This plaque of red gold shows Tutankhamun as the all-conquering hero.

MAKE A GOLDEN FLY

You will need: card, pencil, ruler, scissors, self-drying clay, pva glue and brush, acrylic paint (gold), gold or white ribbon (40cm long x 1cm wide), water pot and brush.

1 Begin by making the body and wings of the fly. Use a ruler and pencil to draw the fly shape onto the card, as shown. Then cut it out carefully with scissors.

2 Next, mould the face of the fly in clay. Roll two small balls for the eyes and outline them with coils of clay. This will make the eyes look larger.

3 Take the card, bend over the tab and glue it down, as shown. This will make a loop. When the fly is finished, ribbon will be threaded through this loop.

BATTLE AXE

This axe has a silver handle and a long blade designed to give a slicing movement. The battle axe was the Egyptian foot soldiers' favourite weapon. Its head of copper or bronze was fitted into a socket or lashed to the wooden handle with leather thongs. Soldiers did not wear armour in battle. Their only protection against weapons such as the heavy axes and spears was large shields made of wood or leather. The mummy of the pharaoh Seqenenre Tao shows terrible wounds to the skull caused by an axe, a dagger and a spear on the battlefield.

The Order of the Golden Fly was a reward for brave soldiers. This is a model of an award given to Queen Aahotep for her part in the war against the Hyksos.

DAGGERS

These ceremonial daggers were found in Tutankhamun's tomb. They are similar to those that would have been used in battle. Egyptian daggers were short and fairly broad. The blades were made of copper or bronze. An iron dagger was also found in Tutankhamun's tomb, but this was very rare. It may have been a gift from the Hittite people, who were mastering the new skill of ironworking.

4 Glue four small strips of white card onto the face, as shown. Push them into the modelling clay. Leave the fly's face in a warm place to dry.

5 Now glue the completed clay fly in place on the card wings. Leave the finished fly to dry for 20 minutes or so before painting it.

6 Carefully paint the fly gold. If your ribbon is white, paint that gold too. Leave the fly and, if necessary, the ribbon to dry. Make two other flies in the same way.

7 Thread the ribbon through the loops in your golden flies, as shown. Originally the golden flies would have been worn on a chain.

Boats and Ships

THE EGYPTIANS were not great seafarers. Their ocean-going ships did sail the Red Sea and the Mediterranean, and may even have reached India, but they mostly kept to coastal waters. However, the Egyptians were experts at river travel, as they are today. They built simple boats from papyrus reed, and these were used for fishing and hunting.

Egypt had little timber, so wooden ships were often built from cedar imported from Lebanon. Boats and model ships were often placed in tombs, and archaeologists have found many well-preserved examples.

The Nile was Egypt's main road, and all kinds of boats travelled up and down. There were barges transporting stones to building sites, ferries taking people across the river, and royal pleasure boats.

THE FINAL VOYAGE

Ships often appear in Egyptian pictures. They were important symbols of the voyage to the next world after death.

ALL ALONG THE NILE

Wooden sailing ships with graceful, triangular sails can still be seen on the river Nile today. They carry goods and people up and down the river. The design of these boats, or *feluccas*, has changed since the time of the ancient Egyptians. The sails on their early boats were tall, upright and narrow. Later designs were broader, like the ones shown above. In Egypt, big towns and cities have always been built along the river, so the Nile has served as an important highway.

MAKE A BOAT

You will need: a large bundle of straw 30cm long, scissors, string, balsa wood, red and yellow card, pva glue and brush.

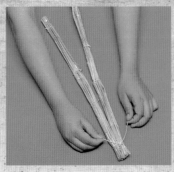

1 Divide the straw into five equal bundles and then cut three of them down to 15cm in length. Tie all five bundles securely at both ends and in the middle, as shown.

2 Take the two long bundles and tie them together at one end as shown. These bundles will form the outer frame of the boat. Put them to one side.

3 Next take the three short bundles of straw and bind them together at both ends. These will form the inner surface of the straw boat.

STEERING ROUND SAND BANKS

This wooden tomb model shows a boat from 1800BC with high curved ends. Long steering oars kept the boat on course through the powerful currents of the flooding river. Although timber was the main material for building larger boats, their designs were similar to those of the simple reed vessels.

SAILING TO ABYDOS

These boats are making a pilgrimage to Abydos. This was the city of Osiris, the god of death and rebirth. Mummies were taken here by boat. Ships and boats played a major part in the religious beliefs of the Egyptians. Ra the Sun god travelled on a boat across the sky. In October 1991, a fleet of 12 boats dating from about 3000BC was found at Abydos near Memphis. The boats were up to 30m in length and had been buried beneath the desert sands. The vessels found in these pits are the oldest surviving large ships in the world.

SIGN OF THE NORTH

The hieroglyph below means boat. It looks a bit like the papyrus reed vessels with their curved ends. This sign later came to mean north. A ship without a sail would always travel north with the current of the Nile.

Early boats were made from papyrus reeds. These were bound with string made from reed fibres.

4 Next push the short bundles into the centre of the long pair firmly. Tie the bundles together with string at one end, as shown.

5 Bring the rear of the long pair of bundles together and tie them securely, as shown. Bind the whole boat together with string.

6 Thread a string lengthwise from one end to the other. The tension on this string should give the high curved prow and stern of your boat.

7 Finally, cut the card and glue it to the balsa sticks to make the boat's paddle and harpoon. Boats like these were used for fishing and hunting hippos.

MESOPOTAMIA

This region between the rivers Tigris and Euphrates, known as "the land between the rivers" is now mostly located in modern Iraq. It was here that farming first developed over 9,000 years ago, and people first learned to read and write, build cities and make laws. Here, too, were the world's first great empires, whose rule stretched over a vast expanse of western Asia. Farmers learned how to irrigate the land, soldiers rode their chariots into battle, and builders raised mighty stone temples called ziggurats. The peoples of Mesopotamia also produced fabulous jewellery in gold and lapis lazuli, and they told marvellous tales of ancient heroes such as Gilgamesh. It is no exaggeration to say that Mesopotamia was the cradle of civilization.

SUMERIAN WORSHIPPERS

Statues of a man and woman from Sumer are shown in an act of worship. The Sumerians were some of the earliest people to live in the south of Mesopotamia. They lived in small, independent cities. At the centre of each city was a temple built as the home for the local god. These two Sumerians had statues made of themselves and put in a temple, so that the god could bless them.

A Land Between Two Rivers

MESOPOTAMIA is the name of an ancient region where some of the world's first cities and empires grew up. Today, most of it lies in modern Iraq. Mesopotamia means 'the land between the rivers' – for the country lay between the Tigris and the Euphrates, two mighty rivers that flowed from the highlands of Turkey in the north down to the Gulf.

The first farmers settled in the low, rolling hills of the north about 9,000 years ago. Here, there was enough rainfall to grow crops and provide pasture for animals. The first cities developed about 3,500 years later, mostly in the flat, fertile flood plains of the south. Rivers and marshes provided water to irrigate crops, plenty of fish, and reeds to build houses and boats. Date palms grew in abundance. At first the south was called Sumer. Later it was known as Babylonia. The land in north Mesopotamia became known as Assyria.

THE WORK OF GIANTS

Most of what we know about the ancient civilizations of Mesopotamia has come from excavations by archaeologists over the last 150 years. In 1845, the British archaeologist Henry Layard unearthed the remains of a once-magnificent palace in the ancient Assyrian city of Nimrud. He found walls decorated with scenes of battles and hunting, and a statue of a human-headed, winged lion so huge that local people were astonished and thought it had been made by giants.

TIMELINE 7000–2100BC

Humans have lived in northern Iraq since the Old Stone Age, when hunter-gatherers lived in caves and rock shelters and made stone tools. Mesopotamian civilization began when people began to settle in villages. They learned how to grow crops and keep animals. Later, city-states grew up, and people developed writing. They became good at building, working metal and making fine jewellery.

painted pottery

7000BC The first villages are established. Edible plants and animals are domesticated, and farming develops. Pottery is made and mud-bricks used for building.

6000BC Use of copper. First mural paintings, temples and seals. Irrigation is used in agriculture to bring water to the fields. Decorated pottery, clay and alabaster figurines. Wide use of brick.

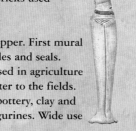

clay figurine

4000BC Larger houses and temples are built. Terracotta sickles and pestles are developed.

writing tablet

3500BC Growth of towns. Development of the potter's wheel, the plough, the first cylinder seals and writing. Bronze, silver and gold worked. Sculptures are made. Trading systems develop.

3000BC Sumerian civilization begins. City-states and writing develop.

7000BC   4000BC   2700BC

TEMPLES OF THE GODS

The ziggurat of Nanna, the Moon god, rises above the dusty plains of modern Iraq. It was once part of the massive temple complex in the city of Ur. Ziggurats showed how clever the Mesopotamians were at building. They were designed as a link between heaven and earth.

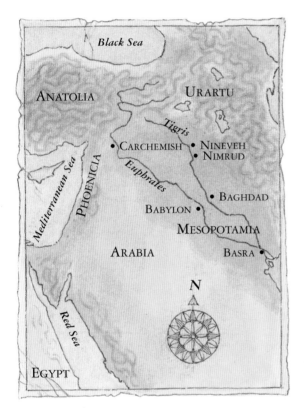

WRITING TABLET

A clay tablet shows an example of some of the earliest writing in the world. The symbols were pressed into a damp clay tablet using a reed pen. The Sumerians originally used writing to keep accounts of goods bought and sold including grain and cattle. Later on, kings used clay tablets as a record of their victories and building activities. Scribes wrote letters, poems and stories about heroes.

POWERFUL NEIGHBOURS

The kingdom of Egypt lay to the south-west of Mesopotamia. In about 2000BC the Assyrians traded with Anatolia in the north-west. They later conquered Phoenician cities in the west and fought Urartu in the north.

Sumerian chariot

2700BC Early Dynastic period. Kings and city administrations rule.

2600BC Royal Standard of Ur made, probably as the sounding box of a lyre.

2500BC Royal Graves of Ur made. Queen Pu-abi and other wealthy individuals buried in tombs with soldiers, musicians and court ladies.

2440BC Inter-state warfare. Kings of Lagash go to war with Umma.

2334BC Sargon of Agade becomes king. He creates the world's first empire, which is maintained by his grandson Naram-sin.

Pu-abi

2200BC The Agade Empire comes to an end. The Gutians, a mountain people, move into Mesopotamia and take some cities.

Ziggurat of Ur-nammu

2141BC Gudea takes the throne of Lagash. Ambitious temple-building programme at Girsu.

2112BC Ur-nammu of Ur tries to re-create the Agade Empire. He builds the famous ziggurat of Ur.

2500BC   2200BC   2100BC

Centres of Civilization

BEFORE THE RISE of the great empires in Mesopotamia, there were many small city-states, each with its own ruler and god. Each state consisted of a city and the surrounding countryside and was the centre of a brilliant civilization. Uruk, in the south, was the first to become important.

Around 2300BC, Sargon, a usurper, conquered all the cities of Mesopotamia and several beyond, creating the world's first empire. After his dynasty died out in about 2150BC, the kings of Ur, a city near the Gulf, tried to re-create Sargon's empire, but with limited success. About 100 years later, Ur fell to the Elamites, invaders from ancient Iran. A nomadic people called the Amorites gradually moved into Mesopotamia and took over the old Sumerian cities, including Babylon, and several of their chiefs became king. The sixth king of Babylon was Hammurabi, famous for his collection of laws.

In the 1500s BC, the Kassites took over Babylonia and ruled well for 400 years. Meanwhile, in the north, the Assyrian Empire had grown from its beginnings in the city-state of Ashur in the third millennium BC. It developed slowly over 2,000 years and reached a glorious peak around 645BC. The empire crumbled when the Babylonians conquered their key cities in 612BC. Babylonia became the most powerful empire in the known world until conquered by the Persian king, Cyrus, in 539BC.

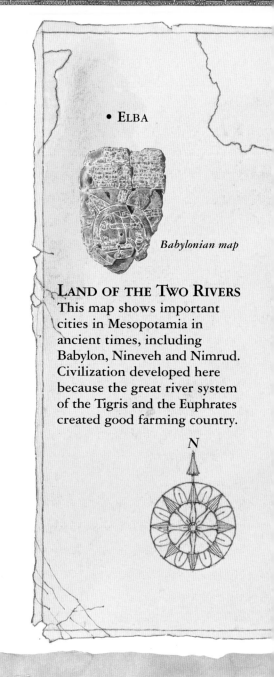

• ELBA

Babylonian map

LAND OF THE TWO RIVERS
This map shows important cities in Mesopotamia in ancient times, including Babylon, Nineveh and Nimrud. Civilization developed here because the great river system of the Tigris and the Euphrates created good farming country.

N

TIMELINE 2050–1000BC

2004BC Ibbi-Sin, last king of Ur, is captured by Elamites and taken to Susa.

2000BC Fall of the Sumerian Empire. Amorites interrupt trade routes. Ur attacked by Elamites and falls. Assyria becomes independent and establishes trading network in Anatolia.

1900BC Amorite chiefs take over some cities as rulers.

1792BC Hammurabi, an Amorite ruler, becomes King of Babylon.

Hammurabi

1787BC King Hammurabi conquers the major southern city of Isin.

1763BC Hammurabi conquers the city of Larsa.

1761BC Hammurabi conquers Mari and Eshnunna and may have conquered the city of Ashur.

1740BC Expansion of the Hittite kingdom in Anatolia, based on the city of Hattusas.

Scorpion man

1595BC The Hittite king, Mursulis, conquers North Syria. Marching further south, he destroys Babylon but does not take over the city.

1570BC The Kassites, a foreign dynasty, begin a 400-year rule of peace and prosperity. King Kurigalzu builds a new capital city, naming it after himself. Babylon becomes a world power on an equal level with the kingdom of Egypt.

2050BC   1790BC   1600BC   1500BC

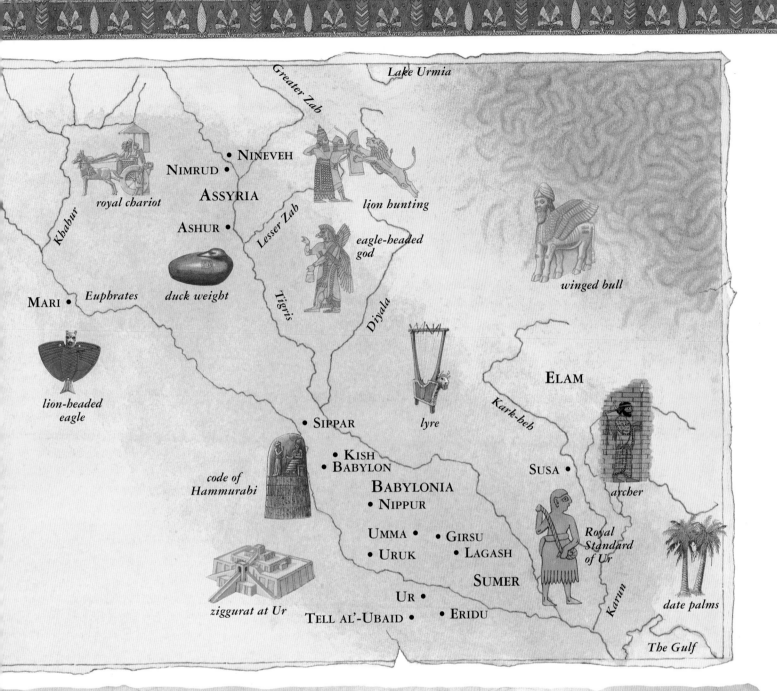

Greater Zab

Lake Urmia

• NINEVEH

NIMRUD •

royal chariot

ASSYRIA

lion hunting

ASHUR •

Lesser Zab

eagle-headed god

Khabur

winged bull

duck weight

Tigris

MARI • *Euphrates*

Diyala

lyre

ELAM

lion-headed eagle

Kark-heh

archer

• SIPPAR

• KISH

• BABYLON

SUSA •

code of Hammurabi

BABYLONIA

• NIPPUR

Royal Standard of Ur

UMMA •

• GIRSU

• URUK

• LAGASH

date palms

SUMER

UR •

ziggurat at Ur

TELL AL'-UBAID •

• ERIDU

Karun

The Gulf

1500BC Mitanni, a new state, develops to the north of Mesopotamia. The people speak Hurrian and fight in two-wheeled horse-drawn chariots. They conquer land from the Mediterranean to the Zagros Mountains, including Assyria.

1365BC Ashur-uballit becomes King of Assyria and gains Assyria's independence from Mitanni.

1150BC The Elamites conquer Babylon, ending Kassite rule.

copper peg

1124BC Nebuchadnezzar I, a later king of Babylon, successfully attacks Elam, bringing back large amounts of booty, including the statue of Marduk, the Babylonian god the Elamites had captured some years earlier.

1115BC Tiglath-pileser I becomes king. He expands Assyrian territory and captures Babylon and other southern cities. First written account of the royal hunt in Mesopotamia. Egyptian king sends him a crocodile as a present.

1076BC Death of Tiglath-pileser I.

1050BC Ashurnasirpal I becomes king.

1000BC Assyria is attacked by many enemies, including the nomadic Aramaeans, who move into Mesopotamia and take over large areas. Their language, Aramaic, and its alphabetic script gradually replace Akkadian and cuneiform.

Humbaba the giant

1130BC   1100BC   1000BC

History Makers

EANNATUM OF LAGASH (C. 2440BC)
A king of Lagash, a city in southern Sumer, who was a great warrior and temple-builder. His victory over the nearby state of Umma was recorded on the Vulture Stela, a limestone carving that showed vultures pecking at the bodies of dead soldiers.

THE NAMES OF Mesopotamian kings are known because their victories and other achievements were recorded on clay tablets and palace wall decorations. The kings wanted to be sure that the gods knew that they had ruled well, and that their names would be remembered for ever. The names of ordinary soldiers and temple builders, the craftsmen who created the beautiful painted wall reliefs and the authors of the sagas and histories were not written down. Some astrologers, army commanders and state officials are known by name because they wrote letters to the king.

SARGON OF AGADE (2334-2279BC)
The man who created the world's first empire, by conquering all the cities of Sumer, Mari and Ebla. He founded the city of Agade, no trace of which has yet been found. A legend tells that when Sargon was a baby, his mother put him in a reed basket and set him afloat on a river. The man who found him trained him to be a gardener. When Sargon grew up, it was believed that he had been favoured by the goddess Ishtar, and he became cup-bearer to the king of Kish (a city north of Babylon).

ENHEDUANNA(C. 2250BC)
The daughter of King Sargon of Agade is one of the few women in Mesopotamian history whose name is known. She held the important post of high priestess to the Moon-god at Ur. Her hymn to the god made her the first known woman author.

TIMELINE 950BC-500BC

911BC Adad-nirari becomes king. Assyria recovers some of her lost possessions and defeats the Aramaeans and Babylon.

879BC Ashurnasirpal II holds a banquet to celebrate the opening of his new palace at Nimrud.

858BC Shalmaneser III, son of Ashurnasirpal II, spends most of his 34-year reign at war, campaigning in Syria, Phoenicia, Urartu and the Zagros Mountains.

Stela of Ashurnasirpal II

c. 845BC Palace of Balawat built.

744BC Tiglath-pileser III brings more territory under direct Assyrian control. Deportation of conquered peoples begins.

721BC Sargon II decorates his palace at Khorsabad with carved reliefs showing his battle victories.

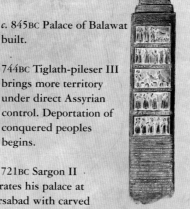
Black obelisk of Shalmaneser III

705BC Sennacherib becomes king of Assyria.

701BC Sennacherib attacks Hezekiah in Jerusalem.

694BC Ashur-nadin-shumi rules Babylon on behalf of his father Sennacherib. He is captured by the Elamites and taken to Susa. In revenge, Sennacherib burns Babylon to the ground.

Balawat Gates

950BC   850BC   710BC   690BC

ASHURBANIPAL OF ASSYRIA (669-631 BC)

A great warrior king, who reigned at the peak of the Assyrian Empire. Ashurbanipal fought successfully against the Elamites, Babylonians and Arabs, and even made Egypt part of his empire for a time. But his greatest gift to civilization was the vast library in his palaces at Nineveh. Here, over 25,000 clay tablets were collected, including letters, legends and astronomical, mathematical and medical works.

HAMMURABI (1792-1750 BC)

The king of Babylon who collected 282 laws concerning family, town and business life and had them recorded on a black stela, a large stone. Other rulers had made laws, but his is the largest collection to survive. The picture shows Shamash, god of justice, giving Hammurabi the symbols of kingship. Towards the end of his reign, he went to war and created an empire, but it did not last long after his death.

NEBUCHADNEZZAR II (604-562 BC)

As crown prince, Nebuchadnezzar fought at the side of his father, the king of Babylon, and brought the Assyrian Empire to an end. Under his own rule, the Babylonians conquered neighbouring countries, such as Palestine, and became one of the world powers of the time. Nebuchadnezzar built great fortifying walls around the city of Babylon and a magnificent ziggurat. He features in the Bible, as the king who captured Jerusalem and sent the people of Judah into captivity.

681BC Sennacherib killed by his eldest son. His youngest son Esarhaddon becomes king.

671BC Esarhaddon invades Egypt and captures the Egyptian capital of Memphis.

668BC Ashurbanipal becomes king of Assyria. His brother Shamash-shum-ukin becomes king of Babylon.

Tiglath-pileser III

664BC Ashurbanipal invades Egypt and destroys the southern city of Thebes.

663 or 653BC Ashurbanipal begins a series of wars with Elam.

652BC Rebellion of Shamash-shum-ukin. Ashurbanipal invades Babylonia.

648BC Ashurbanipal lays siege to Babylon, which suffers starvation.

Nimrud

631BC Death of Ashurbanipal. Assyrian Empire begins to collapse.

612BC Babylonians attack and burn the Assyrian cities of Nimrud and Nineveh.

605BC Assyrians defeated by the Babylonians at the battle of Carchemish.

Ashurbanipal on horseback

604BC Nebuchadnezzar II becomes King of Babylon, and Babylon becomes a world power.

562BC Nebuchadnezzar II dies.

539BC Cyrus of Persia takes Babylon.

663BC   620BC   500BC

A Legendary King

THE ADVENTURES of one king of ancient Sumer were so exciting that they became the subject of some of the oldest stories in the world. Gilgamesh was king of Uruk, one of the most important cities of ancient Sumer, probably around 2700BC. He was said to be two-thirds god and one-third human and seems to have become a legend in his own lifetime. His deeds were first written down about 4,000 years ago and recounted in stories and poems over many generations, passing from the Sumerians to the Babylonians and Assyrians. Finally, in the 7th century BC, the Assyrians wove the individual tales together into an exciting adventure story called an epic and wrote it down on clay tablets. The *Epic of Gilgamesh* was stored in the great libraries of King Ashurbanipal of Assyria, where it was discovered by archaeologists over 100 years ago.

Gilgamesh was not a good king at first, so the gods created Enkidu, a wild, hairy man, to fight him. The king realized he had met his match, and the two then became good friends and went everywhere together.

GIANT ATTACK

The giant Humbaba guarded the Cedar Forest, far away, in Lebanon. His voice was like thunder, his breath was fire, and he could hear the faintest noise from far away. To test their courage, Gilgamesh and Enkidu decided to kill this monster. They were terrified by the giant's dreadful face and taunting words, but finally cut off his head with one stroke.

THE BULL OF HEAVEN

Ishtar, the goddess of love and war (on the left), tries to stop Enkidu and Gilgamesh from killing the Bull of Heaven. Ishtar had fallen in love with the hero-king, and she wanted to marry him. Gilgamesh knew that the goddess was fickle, and turned her down. Ishtar was furious and asked her father, Anu the sky god, to give her the Bull of Heaven so she could take revenge on Gilgamesh. The Bull was a deadly beast who had the power to bring death and long-term misery to the city of Uruk. The two friends fought and killed the bull. Enkidu (on the right) hung on to its tail, as Gilgamesh delivered the death blow with his sword.

THE CITY OF URUK

There is very little of Uruk left today, but it was a very important city when Gilgamesh was king. The city had splendid temples dedicated to Anu, the sky god, and his daughter Ishtar who fell in love with Gilgamesh. The king also built a great wall round the city. When his friend Enkidu died, Gilgamesh was heartbroken, and also frightened because he realized he would die one day, too. He wanted to live for ever. In the end, he decided that creating a beautiful city was his best chance of immortality. He would be remembered for ever for creating the fine temples and massive walls of Uruk.

LASTING FAME

The figures on this stone vase from Uruk probably show Gilgamesh. The king found the lasting fame he wanted because his name lived on in stories and legends, and in statues and carvings such as this.

THE PLANT OF ETERNAL LIFE

A massive stone carving of a heroic figure found in the palace of King Sargon II may be of Gilgamesh. The hero set out to find Utnapishtim, the ruler of another Sumerian city who was said to have found the secret of eternal life. The way was long and dangerous, and led into the mountains where lions prowled. The moon god protected Gilgamesh and led him to a great mountain, with a gate guarded by scorpion men. After a terrifying walk in total darkness, Gilgamesh emerged on the other side of the mountain into the garden of the gods. Beyond the garden were the Waters of Death, but our hero found a ferryman to take him safely across. At last he met Utnapishtim, who told him he would never die if he found a plant that grew on the sea bed. Gilgamesh tied stones on his feet, dived into the sea and picked the plant. However, on the way home, he stooped down to drink at a pool. A water snake appeared and snatched the plant. With it went Gilgamesh's hope of immortality.

The Development of Writing

MESOPOTAMIA WAS ONE OF the first places in the world to develop writing. The earliest examples are about 5,000 years old and come from the Sumerian city-state of Uruk. At first, writing was in the form of pictures and numbers, as a useful way to make lists of produce such as barley, wine and cheese, or numbers of cattle and donkeys. Gradually, this picture-writing was replaced by groups of wedge-shaped strokes, arranged in different ways. This type of writing is called cuneiform, which means 'wedge-shaped', because of the shape the reed pen made as it was pressed into the clay. To begin with, cuneiform writing was only used to write Sumerian, but later it was adapted to write several other languages, including Assyrian and Babylonian.

CLAY TABLET

Writing was done on clay tablets with a stylus (pen) made from a reed. The writer pressed the stylus into a slab of damp clay. This was left to dry and harden. The clay tablet in the picture, from around 3000BC, has symbols on it. One symbol looks like a hand, and others resemble trees or plants. It is not clear which language they represent, although it is likely to be Sumerian.

TWO SCRIBES

The scribe on the right is writing on a clay tablet with a stylus. He is making a list of all the booty and prisoners that his king has captured in battle. He is writing in Akkadian, one of the languages used by the Assyrians. The other scribe is writing on a leather roll, possibly in Aramaic, another language the Assyrians used. Aramaic was an easier language to write because it used an alphabet, unlike Akkadian, which used about 600 different signs.

SHAPES AND SIZES

Differently shaped clay tablets, including prisms and cylinders, were used for writing. Many tablets were flat but some were three-dimensional and hollow like vases. One like this, that narrows at each end, is called a prism. It is about 30cm long and records the military campaigns of King Sargon of Assyria.

A CLAY TABLET

You will need: pen, stiff card, ruler, scissors, modelling clay, cutting board, rolling pin, blunt knife, paper, paint and paintbrush, cloth.

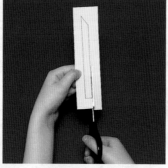

1 Draw a pointed stylus 20cm by 1.5cm on to the stiff card with the pen. Use the shape in the picture as a guide. Cut the shape out with the scissors.

2 Roll out the clay on the cutting board with the rolling pin until it measures about 30cm by 15cm. Use the knife to cut out the clay as shown.

3 Take your card stylus and start writing cuneiform script on your clay tablet. Use the wedge shape of your stylus to make the strokes.

WRITING DEVELOPMENT

Cuneiform signs gradually came to be used for ideas as well as objects. At first, a drawing of a head meant simply 'head', but later it came to mean 'front' and 'first'. The symbols also came to represent spoken sounds and could be used to make new words. For example, in English, you could make the word 'belief' by drawing the symbols for a bee and a leaf. The chart shows how cuneiform writing developed. On the top row are simple drawings. In the middle row the pictures have been replaced by groups of wedges, and in the bottom row are the even more simplified versions of the signs.

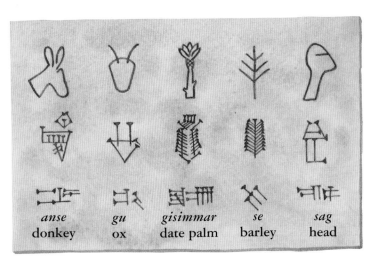

| *anse* | *gu* | *gisimmar* | *se* | *sag* |
| donkey | ox | date palm | barley | head |

WRITING ON THE ROCK FACE

Henry Rawlinson, a British army officer who helped decipher cuneiform in the mid-1800s, risks his life climbing a cliff face at Behistun to copy the writing there. The inscription was in three languages, Old Persian, Elamite and Babylonian (Akkadian). He guessed that the cuneiform signs in Old Persian represented letters of the alphabet and found the name of Darius, the King of Persia. This helped scholars work out all three languages.

The tablet you have made is about half the size of the original. Flat tablets were used for everything from scholarly works on medicine and mathematics to dictionaries and stories. The Epic of Gilgamesh *took up 12 large tablets. Letters were written on tiny tablets.*

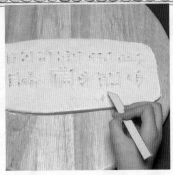

4 Copy the wedge shapes of the cuneiform script shown here. See how each group of strokes combines to make a particular letter or word.

5 Move your tablet on to a piece of clean paper. Take the paintbrush and paint and cover the clay, working the paint well into the cuneiform script.

6 When the painting is finished, wipe across the clay with the cloth. Most of the paint should come off, leaving the lettering a darker colour.

7 Leave the clay and the paint to dry. The lettering on your finished tablet reads:
Nebuchadnezzar
King of Babylon

Seals and Impressions

A SEAL IS A small piece of a hard material, usually stone, with a raised or sunken design on it. When this design is rolled across soft clay, it leaves an impression in the clay. In Mesopotamia, seals were impressed on to lumps of clay that sealed jars of wine or oil. Sometimes the clay was attached to ropes which tied up boxes or baskets. Seals were also rolled across clay writing tablets and their clay envelopes. Impressions in the clay identified who owned the object and made it harder to pass on stolen goods. Seals were often worn as jewellery, as part of a necklace or worn like a brooch. People thought seals also had magical powers that would protect them from illness and other dangers. They sometimes included pictures of the gods for added protection.

PERSONAL STAMP
This is the base of a long cylinder-shaped seal. It also has a design which the owner could use to stamp his or her mark on to objects. The base of a cylinder might only be 1cm in diameter, which made cylinders very hard to carve. Perhaps this seal once belonged to a priest since it shows a priest performing a ritual.

MIRROR IMAGE
A design showing a king or official being led by a goddess into the presence of a great god was a common design on cylinder seals. The design was cut into the seal the opposite way round to the way it would look when it was rolled out.

ROLLING DESIGN
Most seals were cylindrical in shape so that designs could be rolled over a clay tablet and repeated several times. This design shows the storm god, Adad, brandishing his special symbol, forked lightning. The seal was made in Babylon around 600BC. It is made of lapis lazuli, and is 12cm long, about four times as long as most cylinder seals.

A CYLINDER SEAL

You will need: cutting board, rolling pin, self-hardening clay, ruler, paintbrush, glue, cardboard roll, scissors, cocktail stick, clay or plasticine.

1 Take the cutting board, rolling pin and self-hardening clay. Carefully roll out the clay until it measures roughly 15cm by 15cm. Trim one edge.

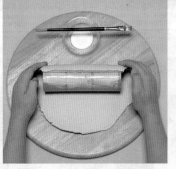

2 Paint glue on to the outside of the cardboard roll. Place the glued roll on to the clay and carefully cover the roll with the clay.

3 Make sure the roll is completely covered with clay. Trim away the excess clay at the edges. Smooth over the join of the clay with your fingers.

ROLL IT OUT

Seals were rolled over clay, so that the design was repeated. Cylinder seals are known from about 3000BC at Uruk, and at Susa in ancient Iran. Various kinds of stone, or glass, bone, shell, ivory or metal were shaped into cylinders. The length of the cylinder was then carved with intricate designs, either hand cut with flint or copper tools, or drilled with bow drills.

SHEEP SEAL

One of the earliest seals ever made comes from the city of Uruk. Its cylindrical base is carved out of a piece of limestone. The sheep-shaped knob on the top is made of copper. Nobody knows who invented the first cylinder seals but some people think they may have been made from the knuckle bones of sheep. Later designs copied the knuckle shape, complete with knobs.

The cylinder seal you have made is very much larger than those used in Mesopotamia. Cylinder seals were usually only 2 or 3cm tall and 1 to 1.5cm in diameter.

4 Use the cocktail stick to mark out a pattern in the clay. When you are happy with your pattern, you will use these marks as guides.

5 Following the marks made with the cocktail stick, use the end of a thin paintbrush to engrave your pattern deeply in the clay. Leave to harden.

6 Take the cutting board and rolling pin again. Roll out the second piece of clay, or plasticine, until it measures roughly 20cm by 14cm.

7 Make sure the clay on your cylinder seal is hard. Roll the seal across the clay or plasticine, pressing down firmly. Watch the pattern appear!

Gods and Goddesses

THE PEOPLE OF MESOPOTAMIA had many gods and goddesses. Every city had a temple to its own chief deity (god), and there were often temples dedicated to other members of the god's family too. The Sumerians and Akkadian-speaking peoples who lived in Mesopotamia worshipped the same gods and goddesses, but had different names for them. The Assyrians and Babylonians also worshipped these gods. The Sumerians called the moon god Nanna, but in Akkadian his name was Sin. The chief Sumerian god was called Enlil, who was often also referred to as King, Supreme Lord, Father, or Creator. According to one Sumerian poem, no one was allowed to look at Enlil, not even the other gods. The Mesopotamian kings believed they had been chosen by Enlil.

The god's chief sanctuary was at the city of Nippur. Legends tell that when the Nippur temple was raided by the army of the King of Agade, Enlil was so angry that he caused the Agade dynasty to come to an end. Enlil owned the Tablets of Destiny, which were thought to control the fates of people and the other gods.

GODDESS
This statue of a goddess was found in pieces at the palace of Mari on the river Euphrates. Two goddesses like her, pouring water from vases, were part of a scene on the walls of the palace courtyard. The painting showed a king being invested with royal power by Ishtar, the goddess of love and war.

BEFORE THE GOD
A scene on a 4,000-year-old seal shows an official called Lamabazi being led into the presence of a great god by a lesser god. The great god is sitting on the throne, and before him is a brazier for burning incense. Lamabazi is holding his hand in front of his face as a sign of respect for the god.

IN THE BEGINNING
Marduk was the god of Babylon. He is shown here standing on his mushushshu (snake dragon). In the *Epic of Creation*, a Babylonian story about how Marduk created the world, he fought against a female monster, Tiamat, and her son, Kingu. After Marduk had killed them, the other gods made him their king. Marduk then brought the rest of creation into existence. He made models of human beings by mixing some clay with the blood of Kingu and then brought them to life.

CLUES TO IDENTITY

Most of our ideas about what the Mesopotamian gods and goddesses looked like come from their pictures on cylinder seals. This one shows Ishtar, the goddess of love and war, carrying her weapons. She is accompanied by a lion, which was her sacred animal. Shamash, the sun god, is recognizable by the flames coming from him, as he rises between two mountains. Ea, the water god, has streams of water gushing from his shoulders.

FERTILE MIND

Nisaba was originally a goddess of fertility and agriculture, although she later became the goddess of writing. Good harvests were very important to the people of Mesopotamia, and almost everyone ate barley bread and dates. This carving of Nisaba shows her covered with plants. She is wearing an elaborate headdress composed of a horned crown and ears of barley. Flowers sprout from her shoulders, and she is holding a bunch of dates.

GOD OF ASSYRIA

Ashur was the chief god of the Assyrians. It was thought that he was the god who chose the Assyrian kings and went before them into battle. He is often symbolized by the same horned cap as Enlil, the chief Sumerian god. Sometimes he is shown standing on a winged bull or on a mushushshu (snake dragon) like Marduk, the god of Babylon. Both gods were honoured in New Year festivals when their priests slapped the reigning king's face, pulled his ears and made him bow low. The king then said he had served his people properly and was re-crowned for another year.

Houses for the Gods

THERE WAS A TEMPLE at the centre of every Mesopotamian city, which was regarded as the house of the local god or goddess. A statue of the deity was put in a special room in the temple, and daily ceremonies were held in his or her honour. One of the main duties of kings was to build or repair temples. King Gudea of Lagash built 15 temples in his city-state. One was inspired by a dream in which the king saw a huge man with two lions and a woman with a writing tablet. Another man appeared with a temple plan, a basket and a brick mould. A dream interpreter told Gudea that the man was the god Ningirsu and the woman was Nisaba, the goddess of writing. This dream meant that Ningirsu wanted Gudea to build him a temple.

TEMPLE BUILDER
King Gudea was one of the great Mesopotamian temple builders. He described the process of building the temple to Ningirsu, near Lagash, on two large clay cylinders. Before installing the god's statue, he purified the temple by surrounding it with fire and anointing the temple platform with aromatic balm. Next day the king washed himself and offered prayers and sacrifices. Finally, the statue was taken to its temple with great ceremony.

FORMER GLORY
All that is left today of the ziggurat (temple-tower) at Ur is the lowest level. In 2100BC it was a three-staged tower built of mud-brick. Three staircases met at the top of the first stage, and the worshippers went on up a single staircase to the temple at the top. Ziggurats may have developed their stepped structure because new temples were often built on top of old ones, and so a huge platform gradually built up. Ziggurats were first built by King Ur-nammu of Ur.

MAKE A ZIGGURAT

You will need: stiff or corrugated card, ruler, pencil, scissors, masking tape, glue, paints and large and small paintbrushes.

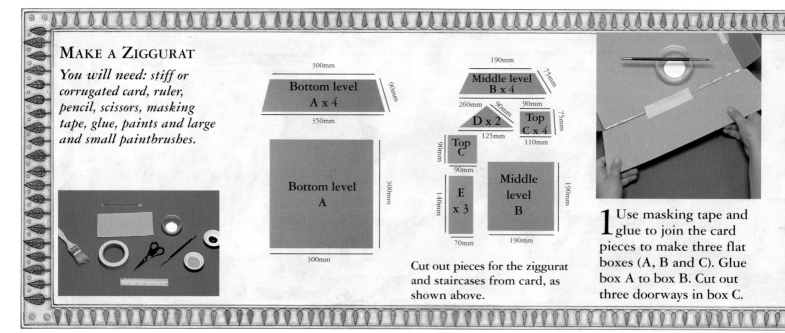

Cut out pieces for the ziggurat and staircases from card, as shown above.

1 Use masking tape and glue to join the card pieces to make three flat boxes (A, B and C). Glue box A to box B. Cut out three doorways in box C.

FOOD FIT FOR THE GODS

The building on this clay impression may be the ziggurat at Babylon, where the seal was found. The figure of a man seems to be offering a sacrifice. The people of Mesopotamia believed they had been created to serve the gods so they gave them special food, including fish, meat, cream, honey, cakes and beer.

THE TOWER OF BABEL

The ziggurat of Marduk, the protector god of Babylon, was thought by modern Westerners to be the Tower of Babel mentioned in the Bible. This is an imaginary picture of the tower the Babylonians built to get closer to heaven. The story says God was angry with them for thinking the way to heaven was so simple. He made the builders speak different languages so they could not understand each other and finish the work.

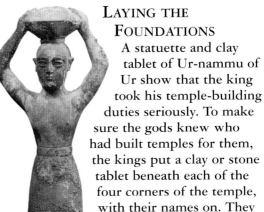

LAYING THE FOUNDATIONS

A statuette and clay tablet of Ur-nammu of Ur show that the king took his temple-building duties seriously. To make sure the gods knew who had built temples for them, the kings put a clay or stone tablet beneath each of the four corners of the temple, with their names on. They often also put statues of themselves like this one, complete with bricks and carrying a brick basket. Ur-nammu built temples at Ur and several other cities.

A real ziggurat was a solid stepped temple-tower of mud-brick. Worshippers climbed the stairways to the god's shrine on the top. It is sometimes seen as a ladder between heaven and earth.

2 Cut out four pieces of card 9 x 2cm, and cut out the edge as shown in the picture. Glue them on top of box C. Then glue box C on top of the ziggurat.

3 Glue triangles D to the first strip E for the main staircase. Cut out two triangles of card for the side stairs and glue them to the other two strips E.

4 Glue the staircases into position as shown. Add strips of card for more doorways and the sides of the main staircase. When dry, paint the ziggurat brown.

5 When completely dry, add details such as the stairs on the staircases and the markings on the sandstone, with black paint and a fine brush.

Sumerian Burial

WHEN the Sumerian city of Ur was excavated in the 1930s, archaeologists found hundreds of graves. The discovery gave an insight into how the inhabitants regarded death and burial. Little evidence about death rituals in other parts of Mesopotamia survives.

In Ur, most people seem to have been buried in family graves under the courtyards of their houses. Their children were put in jars and placed in chapels above the family graves. Other people were buried in the city cemetery. Most bodies had been wrapped in reed mats or placed in baskets (which no longer existed but the patterns of their weaving were pressed into the soil). Most people had a few belongings buried with them, but 17 of the graves contained many precious objects. They may have belonged to kings and queens, and so were called the Royal Graves.

FIT FOR THE QUEEN'S COURT
A headdress of gold and semi-precious stones, with finely worked golden leaves and ribbons, was found in the grave of Queen Pu-abi at Ur. It may have belonged to one of the ladies of her court. The body of the queen herself was bedecked in gold earrings, finger rings and necklaces. Tiny threads of wool suggested that she had been wrapped in a red woollen cloak.

CEREMONIAL HELMET
An exquisitely decorated helmet of electrum (a mixture of gold and silver) may have belonged to Meskalamdug, whose name was found on two golden bowls in the grave. The wig-like pattern is hammered from the inside. The holes around the edge were provided so that a lining could be sewn in to make it more comfortable.

RAM IN THE THICKET
No one knows why this ram was placed in a mass grave called the Great Death Pit. A pair of rams or goats in a thicket was a common image in Mesopotamian art. This ram was one of a pair. It was made of wood decorated with bright blue lapis lazuli to show the animal's hairy coat and a silver plate over its belly.

A GOLD HELMET
You will need: balloon, flour, water and newspaper to make papier mâché, scissors, card 60cm by 20cm, masking tape, pen, pieces of white cotton fabric, glue, string, gold and black paint and paintbrushes.

1 Blow up the balloon until it is as big as your head. Dip newspaper strips in flour-and-water paste, and cover the balloon with layers of papier mâché.

2 When the papier mâché is completely dry, pop the balloon. Trim the edge of the helmet. Attach the piece of card to the helmet with masking tape.

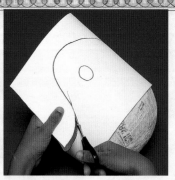

3 With the pen, draw the shape of the sides of the helmet as shown. Cut round the shape with the scissors. Draw and cut out holes for the ears.

ROYAL FUNERAL

The bodies of six guards and 68 court ladies were found in a grave at Ur called the Great Death Pit. Woolley thought they were the servants of kings and queens who had been chosen to accompany them to the afterlife. They walked down into the grave in a great funeral procession. Then they drank a drugged drink and fell asleep never to wake again.

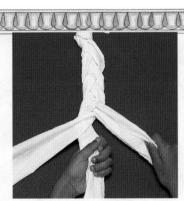

You have made a copy of Meskalamdug's ceremonial helmet. One meant for real use would have been made of a stronger metal such as copper.

GOLDEN TABLEWARE

So many beautiful golden objects, such as these fluted bowls and tumblers, were found in certain graves at Ur that Woolley called them the Royal Graves. In 1989, the tombs of some Assyrian queens were found under the palace floor at Nimrud. The queens were buried with their exquisite jewellery of gold, but unlike Queen Pu-abi of Ur they were not buried with their servants.

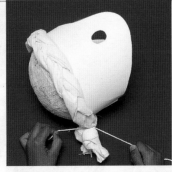

4 Take three strips of white fabric 100cm by 4cm. Tie them together with a knot at one end and plait the three strips loosely and knot the other end.

5 Glue the plait around the helmet, covering the join between the papier mâché and card as shown. Tie off the end with string to make a tail.

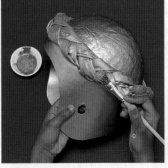

6 Paint the whole helmet, inside and out, with gold paint. Use a broad paintbrush. Paint over the cloth plait, too. Allow the paint to dry thoroughly.

7 Add detail of hair to the helmet using the black paint and a fine paintbrush. You can use Meskalamdug's helmet to give you some ideas!

Education

SCHOOL BUILDINGS in Mesopotamia looked very similar to ordinary houses. Archaeologists have been able to identify the schools because large numbers of clay tablets containing mistakes and corrections were found there. The tablets had been corrected by the teachers just as modern teachers mark books. A school was called edubba, which means tablet house.

The tablets show which subjects were taught and how schools were run. The headteacher was called ummia (expert), but was also known as the school father. The teachers' job was to write out tablets for students to copy, to correct their exercises and listen to them recite what they had learned by heart.

The school day was very long, lasting from sunrise to sunset. Discipline was very strict. One boy was caned several times in one day – for getting his clothes in a mess, making a mistake on his tablet and talking in class.

MUSIC LESSONS
Students learned music at school. In examinations they were asked questions about playing musical instruments, different types of songs and how to conduct a choir. This figure showing a man playing a lyre is on a highly decorated box called the Royal Standard of Ur because it was once thought it was a standard that was carried into battle.

LEARNING ABOUT HEROES
When students were good at reading and writing, they studied the Mesopotamian myths and legends, such as the stories of the heroic king of Uruk, Gilgamesh, and his friend Enkidu.

CIVIL SERVANT
Ebih-il was Superintendent of the Palace at Mari. The main aim of schools was to produce scribes and civil servants like Ebih-il. Some students became scholars who worked in the temple and royal libraries, or teachers. At school, boys learned the two main languages, Sumerian and Akkadian, by copying and learning by heart groups of related words. They also studied other subjects, such as botany and zoology, by copying out lists of plants, animals, insects and birds.

EXCLUSIVE EDUCATION
If these modern-day Iraqi boys had been born 5,000 years ago, they would probably not have gone to school. Only boys from well-off families went to school in ancient Mesopotamia. They were the sons of high-up officials, officers in the army, sea captains or scribes.

PLAYING WITH NUMBERS

Maths was very important in Mesopotamian schools. Clay tablets, such as this one, had mathematical problems written on them. Some of these related to practical matters, but most were just brain-teasers. The Mesopotamians obviously liked playing with numbers. Students also had tables for multiplying and dividing, and for working out squares and square roots. There were two number systems, one using 10 as a base and the other, 60. We use 10 as a base too, and 60 to measure time, for example.

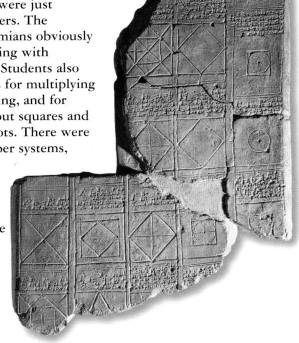

LUNCH BOX
A schoolboy's lunch box might be packed with unleavened bread cakes made from barley flour, and some cheese. Cheese was made from skimmed milk and was quite cheap to produce. His mother would put in some dates to give him energy. Sometimes for a treat he might have an apple or a pear.

curd cheese

dates

bread

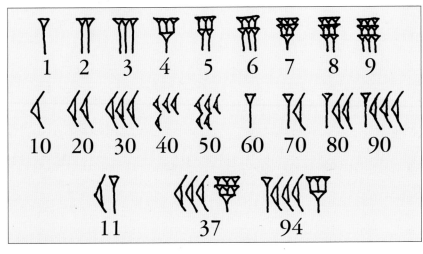

WRITING NUMBERS

This chart shows how numbers were written in Mesopotamia. Numbers were written on clay tablets using a system of wedge-shaped signs. For the numbers 1 to 9 the appropriate number of wedges was arranged in groups. 10 was one slanting wedge, 20 two slanting wedges, and so on up to 50. The figure 60 was written with an upright wedge. There was no sign for zero. The same symbol is used for the numbers 1 and 60. You can tell which number is which by looking at the order of the wedges. For example, if the slanting wedge comes first the number is 11 (10+1). If the slanting wedge comes afterwards the number is 70 (60+10).

PRINCE'S EDUCATION

Learning to drive a chariot and fight in battle were part of King Ashurbanipal's education when he was crown prince. Officials taught him the Sumerian and Akkadian languages, which he found difficult. He also studied multiplication and division, astronomy and ancient literature, and learned to ride a horse and hunt.

Music and Games

SEVEN-STRINGED HARP
Harps and lyres were two of the most popular musical instruments in Mesopotamia. They were sometimes played in funeral processions. The harp on this Babylonian terracotta relief has seven strings, which were probably made from animal gut.

INSTRUMENTAL MUSIC and singing played an important part in Mesopotamian life. Musicians entertained at the court of the king and played in temple rituals. King Gudea of Lagash wrote a learned work about music. Most of the musical works that have come down to us are hymns to gods and kings. For example, we know that Sargon of Agade's daughter, Enheduanna, composed a hymn to the moon god at Ur. People may have amused themselves with music, singing and dancing in their homes and in the market place. One Sumerian poem about the goddess Inanna and her lover Dumuzi speaks about them going to see an entertainer singing and dancing in the public square. In the Middle East today, musicians and storytellers still entertain in the open squares of cities.

ROYAL GAME OF UR
A beautiful board game was found in the Royal Graves of Ur. It is made from wood covered in bitumen (tar) and decorated with a mosaic of shell, bone, blue lapis lazuli, red glass and pink limestone. The game may have been a bit like Ludo, with two sets of counters and four-sided dice, but the rules have not been found!

SINGING STAR
Ur-Nanshe was the chief singer at the court of King Iblul-il at Mari. The singers of Mari were famous throughout Mesopotamia and beyond. The figure may have once held a harp.

MAKE A LYRE

You will need: pencil, card, scissors, 3 pieces of dowel 55cm long, masking tape, glue, flour, water and newspaper for papier mâché, sandpaper, paints and paintbrushes, pins, piece of balsa wood, string or elastic.

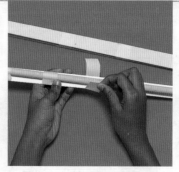

1 Draw a bull shape 40cm long by 25cm wide on to the card, following the shape shown above. You will need two of these card cutouts. Cut out two horns.

2 Cut four card strips 3cm by 55cm. Use masking tape and glue to attach a strip to each side of two of the pieces of dowel.

3 Fix the two dowel pieces to one of the bull shapes, one coming out of the head, the other out of the rump. Tape the other bull shape on top.

DRUMS AND CYMBALS

Musicians pictured on a palace wall are playing cymbals and a drum as well as stringed instruments. There were several kinds of drums in Babylonia. One was the balag, which was shaped like an hour-glass. It was used in temple rituals to soothe the gods. Another was the lilissu, which was set up in temple courtyards and beaten when there was an eclipse of the Moon. Flutes were also played. Just over a hundred years ago a Babylonian clay whistle was found. Unfortunately it has now been lost.

CEREMONY WITH MUSIC

Musicians play in victory celebrations. They are playing at a ceremony to celebrate King Ashurbanipal's victory over the King of Elam. Musicians took part in other rituals too, such as one after a lion hunt when Assyrian kings offered the dead animals to the gods.

Your lyre is like one found in the Royal Graves of Ur. It was made of wood and decorated with a mosaic in shells, blue lapis lazuli and limestone. The bull's head was made of gold and lapis lazuli with ivory horns. It had 11 strings.

4 Use masking tape to attach the horns. Make a flour-and-water paste and use papier mâché to fill the gap between the two bull shapes and cover the bull.

5 Take the third piece of dowel and tape to the top of the other two pieces. Smooth with sandpaper and paint. Add cardboard pegs as shown and paint.

6 When the papier mâché is dry, decorate the body of the lyre with the paints. Use different coloured paints to create an inlaid mosaic effect.

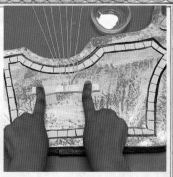

7 Cut 7 strings from string or elastic. Tie them to the balsa wood and pin it on the bull's body. Tie the other end of the strings to the top piece of dowel.

Family Life

LIFE WAS HARD for ordinary families in Mesopotamia. Many babies and young children died from disease or because of poor maternity care. Boys from poorer families did not go to school but worked with their fathers, who taught them their trades. Girls stayed at home with their mothers and learned how to keep house and look after the younger children. Some of the details of family life are described in ancient clay tablets. In one tablet, a boy rudely tells his mother to hurry up and make his lunch. In another one, a boy is scared of what his father will say when he sees his bad school report.

In some ways, Mesopotamian society was quite modern. The law said that women could own property and get a divorce. However, if a woman was unable to have a baby, she had to agree to her husband taking a second wife. The second wife and her children had rights too. They remained part of the household even if the first wife had a child after all.

MOTHERHOOD
Having lots of healthy children, especially sons, was very important because families needed children to grow up and work for them. Most women stayed at home to look after their families. Women did not usually go out to work, but some had jobs as priestesses. Some priestesses were single but others were married women.

HOUSEHOLD GOODS
Pottery was used in Mesopotamian homes from the time of the first villages. At first it was hand-made, but later a potter's wheel was used. This pottery jug may have been modelled on a jug made of metal. Tools and utensils were made of stone or metal. There was not much furniture in a Mesopotamian house, just mud-brick benches for sitting or sleeping on. There may have been rugs and cushions to make the homes more homely and comfortable, but none have survived.

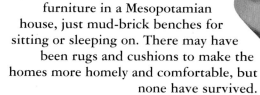

MODEL HOUSE
From models such as this one, we know that homes in Mesopotamia were similar to village houses in modern Iraq. They were built of mud-brick and were usually rectangular, with rooms around a central courtyard. Doors and windows were small to keep the house warm in the cold winters, and cool during the hot summers. Flat roofs, reached by stairs from the central court, could be used as an extra room in summer.

MESOPOTAMIAN FASHIONS

A statue of a worshipper found in a temple shows the dress of a Sumerian woman. Dresses were of sheepskin, sometimes with a sheepskin shawl as well, or of woollen cloth. One shoulder was left bare. Some women, who may have been priestesses, wore tall, elaborate hats like this one. Later fashions included long, fringed garments. Sumerian men wore sheepskin kilts, but men in the Assyrian and Babylonian Empires wore long, woollen tunics. Both sexes wore jewellery.

EARNING A LIVING

Most families in ancient Mesopotamia depended on agriculture for a living, just as many people in the Middle East do today. Farmers rented their land from bigger landowners, such as important officials, kings or temples, and had to pay part of what they produced in taxes. Many townspeople had jobs in local government or worked in the textile and metalwork industries.

BUILD IT UP

Mud-bricks are made from a mixture of clayey mud and straw mixed with water. The straw stops the bricks from cracking. The mixture is put in square or oblong moulds and left to dry in the sun for several weeks. The bricks are usually made in the summer after the harvest, when there is plenty of straw available and it is less likely to rain (which would damage the bricks).

straw

clay

GONE FISHING

There were lots of fish in the rivers and fishponds of ancient Iraq, and fish seem to have been an important part of people's diet. Fishbones were found at Eridu, in the south of Sumer, in the oldest level of the temple. Perhaps fish were offered to the water god Enki as an offering. (He is the god with streams of water containing fish springing out of his shoulders.) Some of the carved reliefs from the Assyrian palaces give us rare glimpses into everyday life and include little scenes of men going fishing.

A Woman's Life

MOST MESOPOTAMIAN WOMEN married in their early teens. Sometimes, two families agreed on a marriage when the future man and wife were still children. After the agreement was made, the children lived with their parents until they were old enough to set up home together. Then the young man took a betrothal present to his bride's family, such as some clothing, some silver and a ring. When the marriage took place, the wife's father would give her a dowry of jewellery, clothes or furniture to take to her new home. She might be given a field or an orchard as her property.

Some women had a lot of responsibility. Queen Shibtu, wife of King Zimri-lim of Mari, ran the palace while her husband was away and kept him informed about everything that went on.

A queen seems to have become important only after producing a son. The mother of a king often had higher status than his wife.

OF ROYAL BLOOD
The fine clothes and jewellery on this statue show that it is a figure of a princess. She belonged to the family of King Gudea of Lagash. Her name was once written on her statue, but unfortunately it can no longer be read. The statue was found at Girsu, where King Gudea built his temples, so she may also have been a priestess.

WOMEN'S RIGHTS
The laws of King Hammurabi of Babylon are carved on this stone pillar. They tell us about some of the legal rights held by women in Mesopotamia. They could own property and engage in business. A woman could get a divorce if her husband treated her badly. If she could prove her innocence, she could reclaim her dowry and return to her parents' home. But if she neglected her duties as a wife, the laws said she could be thrown into water.

MAKE A NECKLACE

You will need: self-hardening clay, cocktail stick, paper, pen, scissors, paintbrushes, glue, paints in bright colours, wire and pliers, strong thread.

1 Make a variety of beads using the self-hardening clay, in long shapes and round shapes. Use the cocktail stick to make a hole through each bead.

2 Cut shapes out of the paper following the pattern shown above. The shapes should be about 3cm long. They will be used to make cylindrical beads.

3 Roll the pieces of paper tightly around a fine paintbrush as shown. Glue the tail of the paper to secure it to itself and leave it to dry.

WOMEN'S WORK

A relief shows a woman spinning. A great deal is known about the women who worked at Mari, a city on the River Euphrates, because they are mentioned in letters that archaeologists found in the palace ruins. Many women worked in the textile industry. There were several female musicians. Other women worked in the royal kitchens, or were midwives who helped mothers in childbirth. The biggest surprise of all was to find that one woman was a doctor.

EDUCATING DUDU

Although usually only boys went to school, a few women were educated and became scribes, such as this woman, Dudu. There were nine women scribes at Mari. Their names appear on ration lists, showing that they were palace employees. We do not know how they trained.

EXPENSIVE NECKLACE

Only a rich woman would have worn a necklace like this, as it would have been quite expensive. The blue lapis lazuli was imported. It was mined in the mountains of Afghanistan and made into beads in workshops in Iran. The necklace was made about 4,500 years ago.

Your necklace would probably have been made of gold, blue lapis lazuli, red carnelian and limestone. People who could not afford these used a glassy material called paste to make beads.

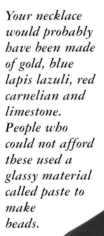

4 When the beads are dry, paint them. If you are using different colours, allow the paint to dry thoroughly between before adding the next coat.

5 Cut two small pieces of wire. Use the pliers to make two hooks. One side of each hook should be closed as shown, the other should be left open.

6 Tie a long piece of strong thread firmly to the closed side of one hook. Push the end of the thread through the painted beads to string the beads.

7 When you get to the end of the thread, or have used up all your beads, attach the end of the thread to the closed end of the second hook.

Farming

Northern Mesopotamia had enough rainfall to let farmers grow crops, but in the dry south farmers had to use the Tigris and the Euphrates rivers to irrigate the land. The main crop was barley. Wooden ploughs were used to break up the soil before the seed was sown with seed drills. A Sumerian almanac or diary told farmers what they should do at various times of the year. Vegetables and fruit were also grown, dates being particularly valued. They also kept cattle, sheep and goats on the grasslands between the cultivated areas. The landscape looked much the same as it does today, although rivers have changed course over the years. The weather has always been unpredictable and sometimes crops are spoiled by sudden storms.

SHEPHERD WITH LAMB
A Sumerian shepherd holds a lamb. Sheep not only provided meat and milk, but the sheepskin garments that were commonly worn. Wool was also woven into cloth to make long tunics, dresses and shawls. People had to pay a proportion of the goods they produced as taxes to the city-states.

FOOD SOURCE
Cows were an important part of the Mesopotamian economy. Many different kinds of cheese and other dairy products are mentioned in clay tablet records. One Sumerian temple frieze shows work in a dairy, with two men churning butter in large jars. Other men are straining a substance from one vessel to another to make cheese.

WATER LIFELINE
Summers in Mesopotamia were very hot and dry. From the earliest settlements in Sumer to present-day Iraq, farmers have dug channels to carry water from the Tigris and Euphrates rivers to their fields. Mesopotamian kings believed that organizing the building of canals was a religious duty.

MAKE A RAM-HEADED DRINKING CUP

You will need: paper cup, newspaper, masking tape, scissors, flour and water to make papier mâché, fork, fine sandpaper, paint and paintbrushes, varnish.

1 Scrunch up a piece of newspaper. Attach the ball of newspaper to the bottom end of the paper cup with pieces of masking tape.

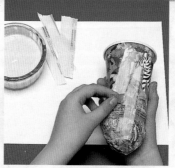

2 Make a paste with water and flour using the fork to mix the paste. Tear strips of newspaper and dip them into the paste, then cover the cup.

3 Twist two pieces of newspaper into coil shapes for the horns and fix them to the cup. Cover the cup inside and out with papier mâché. Leave to dry.

A HEALTHY DIET

By looking at ancient seeds, archaeologists have been able to find out what people ate in the past. The Mesopotamians ate fruit and vegetables such as apples, pomegranates, medlars and grapes, onions, leeks and turnips. The country's most important crop was barley, which was used for making bread and beer. Wheat was grown to a lesser extent. Barley was made into a porridge-like mixture flavoured with cumin, mustard, coriander and watercress.

apples   *medlars*

grapes   *pomegranates*

DATE ORCHARDS

Some of the biggest date orchards in the world are in the south of modern Iraq. The fruits were important in ancient times because they were an excellent source of energy. Dates could be dried and stored so that they were available all the year round, and were made into wine. Date syrup was used as a sweetener.

Animal-headed cups for drinking wine have been found at Nimrud. Your cup is copied from a pottery one. Wealthy people also used cups of bronze.

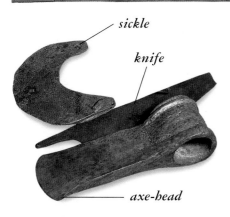

sickle

knife

axe-head

ANCIENT TOOLS

Agricultural tools were made of copper and bronze, and included axe-heads, knives and sickles for harvesting. Ancient farmers also had seed drills and wooden ploughs drawn by oxen, like the ones still used today, although many modern farmers also use tractors.

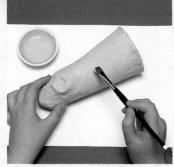

4 When the papier mâché is completely dry, smooth it down with sandpaper. Paint the whole cup in a creamy beige colour.

5 When the base coat is dry, use a fine paintbrush and brown paint to add details to your cup. Paint in the ram's horns and face.

6 Use red paint to add stripes to your drinking cup. Paint three red stripes around the neck, and two red stripes around the open end.

7 When the paint is completely dry, coat the drinking cup with a water-based varnish. Allow the first coat to dry before applying a second coat.

Science and Technology

THE PEOPLE OF MESOPOTAMIA developed many different aspects of technology including metalworking, pottery, glassmaking, the manufacture of textiles and leatherworking. They were also experts at irrigation and flood control, building elaborate canals, water storage and drainage systems. They were among the first people in the world to use metal. An early copper sculpture, made in 2600BC, comes from the temple of Ubaid near Ur. It shows a lion-headed eagle clutching two stags in its talons. The armies used vast amounts of bronze for their weapons and armour. King Sennacherib used striding lions, cast in solid bronze and weighing hundreds of kilograms, to support the wooden pillars of his palace at Nineveh.

SUPPLYING THE CITY
Water wheels and aqueducts such as these are still used in the Middle East today. The Assyrians built aqueducts to take water to the cities to meet the needs of their growing populations. The Assyrian king Sennacherib (701-681BC) had 10km of canals cut from the mountains to the city of Nineveh. He built dams and weirs to control the flow of water, and he created an artificial marsh, where he bred wild animals and birds.

A WEIGHTY CHALLENGE
Workers in a quarry near the Assyrian city of Nineveh prepare to move an enormous block of stone roughly hewn in the shape of a lamassu (human-headed winged bull). The stone is on a sledge carried on wooden rollers. At the back of the sledge, some men have thrown ropes over a giant lever and pull hard. This raises the end of the sledge and other workers push a wedge underneath. More workers stand ready to haul on ropes at the front of the sledge. At a signal everyone pulls or pushes and the sledge moves forward.

MAKE A PAINTED PLATE
You will need: a plate, flour, water and newspaper to make papier mâché, scissors, pencil, fine sandpaper, ruler, paints and paintbrushes.

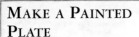

1 Tear strips of newspaper and dip them in the water. Cover the whole surface of the plate with the wet newspaper strips.

2 Mix up a paste of flour and water. Cover the newspaper strips with the paste. Allow to dry, then add two more layers, leaving it to dry each time.

3 When the papier mâché is dry, trim around the plate to make a neat edge. Remove the plate. Add more papier mâché to strengthen the plate.

MAKING CLOTH

Spinning and weaving were usually done by women in the home or in state or temple factories. Large herds of sheep and goats were kept to produce wool, to make clothing. Flax was grown for its fibres, which were used to make linen as early as 3000BC. Cotton was not introduced until the reign of Sennacherib in the 700s BC.

wool

sheep's wool

sheep's fleece

METALWORKERS

Ceremonial daggers demonstrate the Sumerians' skill at working with gold. Real weapons would have had bronze blades. The Sumerians cast metal by making a wax model of the object required which they covered with clay to make a mould. A small hole in the side let the wax escape when it was heated, so that molten metal could be poured into the mould. When the metal cooled, the mould was broken and the object removed.

You have copied a plate from Tell Halaf, a small town where some of the finest pots in the ancient world were made. They were decorated with orange and brown paints made from oxides found in clay.

HAND-MADE VASES

Vases found in Samarra in the north of Mesopotamia were produced about 6,000 years ago. They were shaped by hand and fired in a kiln, then painted with geometric designs. Later, a wheel like a turntable was used to shape the clay, which speeded up the process.

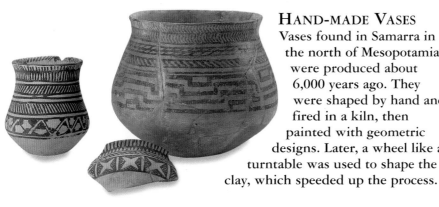

4 When the papier mâché is completely dry, smooth it down with fine sandpaper. Then paint the plate on both sides with a white base coat.

5 When the paint is dry, use a pencil and ruler to mark a dot in the centre of the plate. Draw four large petals around this point and add details as shown above.

6 When you are happy with your design, paint in the patterns using three colours for the basic pattern. Allow each colour to dry before adding the next.

7 Add more detail to your plate, using more colours, including wavy lines around the edge. When you have finished painting, leave it to dry.

Travel by Land and Water

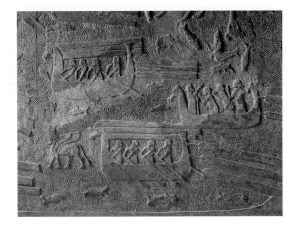

THE TIGRIS AND EUPHRATES rivers and their tributaries provided a very good communications network around the country, so most people travelled by boat rather than on foot. In the south, boats were made of reeds, and were very convenient for getting about in the marshy areas at the head of the Gulf. Once the wheel had been introduced, some wealthy people travelled by horse and chariot along roads and local tracks. Chariots were mainly used by the Assyrian kings and their courtiers when hunting and in battle. At rivers, the chariots were dismantled and carried across on boats. The soldiers swam across using inflated animal skins as lifebelts. The horses had to get over as best they could.

TRANSPORTING LOGS
Phoenician ships tow logs of cedar wood along the Mediterranean coast. There was no wood in Assyria that was suitable for the palace roofs, so cedar was imported from Phoenicia. When they reached land, the logs were dragged overland on sledges. Once they reached the rivers, the timber could be floated again. Heavy goods were also often transported on rafts supported by inflated animal skins.

BEST FOOT FORWARD
People without transport had to walk, but everyone travelled by boat or cart whenever possible. Conquered people often travelled hundreds of kilometres from their original homes to new ones in Assyria and Babylonia. These people have been conquered by the Assyrians, and they are taking heavy bales of woollen cloth as a tribute to their new king. Armies marched vast distances too, wearing high leather boots. King Nebuchadnezzar I of Babylon led his armies on a gruelling march to Susa at the height of summer to recapture the statue of Marduk, the chief god of Babylon.

MAKE A BOAT
You will need: cutting board, modelling clay, piece of dowel about 20cm long, cocktail stick, paints and paintbrushes, glue, varnish and brush, string, scissors.

1 Make an oval dish shape out of the clay. It should measure 14cm long by 11cm wide by 4cm deep. Make a mast hole for the dowel and attach it to the base.

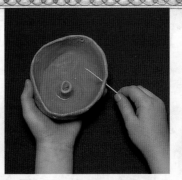

2 Trim round the top of the boat to neaten it. Use the cocktail stick to make four holes through the sides. Leave the boat to dry out completely.

3 Paint the boat all over with a light brown base colour. Then using a brush and your finger, flick contrast colours to create a mottled effect.

SEAFARING NATION

The Phoenicians of the eastern Mediterranean, whose cities were conquered by the Assyrian kings, were the great sailors and shipbuilders of the time. They traded fine ivory and metal work, and richly coloured woollen cloth, throughout the Mediterranean and beyond. The ships were large and many-oared, and the sailors worked out how to navigate by the stars. The Phoenicians may have been the first people to sail around Africa – via the Strait of Gibraltar, the southern tip of Africa, and along the east coast to the Red Sea.

OVERLAND EXCURSIONS

By about 900BC, spoked wheels had replaced the earlier wheels made from a single piece of solid wood. In Sumerian times, onegars (wild asses) hauled chariots, while oxen and mules were used for heavy goods. Traders carried their goods on long caravans (lines) of donkeys that were sturdy enough to travel long distances. From about 900BC the Assyrians used camels as well. Local roads were little more than tracks, but messengers and state officials sped on horseback along the well-maintained roads between the main centres of the Assyrian Empire.

Small boats are still used today on the River Euphrates. Your boat is based on a model clay boat from 4000BC. It has a mast for a light sail. It might have been steered using oars or a punt pole.

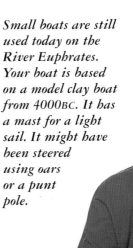

4 Put a blob of glue inside the mast hole. Put more glue around the end of the dowel and push it into the hole. This is your mast.

5 Wait until the glue has dried and the mast is firm. Then paint a layer of water-based varnish all over the boat. Leave to dry and repeat.

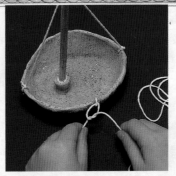

6 Take two lengths of string about 60cm long. Tie the end of one piece through one of the holes, around the top of the mast and into the opposite hole.

7 Complete the rigging of the boat by tying the other piece of string through the empty holes and around the top of the mast as before. Trim the strings.

Banking and Trade

THE PEOPLE OF MESOPOTAMIA were very enterprising and expert business people. They travelled long distances to obtain goods they needed, importing timber, metal and semi-precious stones.

Around 2000BC, the Assyrians had a widespread, long-distance trading network in Anatolia (modern Turkey). The headquarters were in the northern Mesopotamian city of Ashur and the trade was controlled by the city government and by large family firms.

The head of a firm usually stayed in Ashur but trusted members of the family were based in Anatolian cities such as Kanesh. From here they conducted business on the firm's behalf, going on business trips around Anatolia, and collecting any debts or interest on loans. Deals were made on a credit basis, for the Assyrian families acted as money-lenders and bankers as well. On delivery, goods and transportation (the donkeys) were exchanged for silver, which was then sent back to Ashur. In about 2000BC, one Kanesh businessman failed to send back the silver, and the firm threatened to send for the police.

TROPHIES AND TAX
Carved ivory furniture, like this panel, and bronze bowls were often carried off after successful battles. There is little evidence of trade in Mesopotamia from 900 to 600BC. The Assyrian kings took anything they wanted from the people they defeated. They collected as tax whatever was needed, such as straw and food for horses.

TRADE TO KANESH
Donkeys or mules are still used to transport goods from one village to another in modern Iraq. When trade with ancient Turkey was at its peak, donkey caravans (lines) took large amounts of tin and textiles through the mountain passes to Kanesh. A typical load for one donkey would usually consist of 130 minas (about 65kg) of tin (which was specially packed and sealed by the city authorities), and ten pieces of woollen cloth.

PRECIOUS THINGS

The marvellous jewellery in the Royal Graves of Ur not only demonstrates the skills of the jewellers who made it, but is also evidence that the Sumerians went in for long-distance trade. None of the materials used to make the jewellery was available in Sumer, so the precious stones had to be imported. The gold may have come from Oman, the lapis lazuli from Afghanistan and the carnelian from the Indus Valley.

semi-precious stones

lapis lazuli

gold

STRIKING A DEAL

Two merchants make a contract. One is agreeing to supply goods for a certain amount of silver, and the other is promising to pay by a certain date. The details of a deal were written on a clay tablet and impressed with the cylinder seals of the two men. Often a copy was made and put in a clay envelope. If there was a dispute about the deal later, the envelope would be broken and the agreement checked.

LETTERS FROM KANESH

The site of the trading settlement of Kanesh, where the Assyrians did an enormous amount of business, has been excavated. A great many clay tablets were found, many of them business letters. From these letters, it is clear that the Anatolian princes had the first pick of the goods brought by Assyrian merchants. They charged the merchants taxes on their donkey caravans. In return, the princes protected the roads and provided insurance against robbers.

CASH AND CARRY

There was no money in Mesopotamia, so goods were usually paid for in silver. Silver was measured in shekels and each shekel weighed about 8g. It was carefully weighed to make sure that the person paying gave an amount equal to the value of the goods bought.

Running the Empire

FROM THE BEGINNING of the 800s BC, the country of Assyria began to grow into a vast empire. The land was divided into provinces, each one named after its main city, such as Nineveh, Samaria, Damascus, or Arpad, each with its own governor. The governor had to make sure that taxes were collected, call up soldiers in times of war, and supply workers when a new palace or temple was to be built. He had to provide safe passage for merchants and was responsible for law and order. If the king and his army passed through the province, the governor supplied them with food and drink. A vast system of roads connected the king's palace with governors' residences and all the important cities of the Empire.

ENFORCED REMOVAL
Conquered people are banished from their homeland to go and live in Assyria. These people were from Lachish, near Jerusalem, and were moved to the Assyrian city of Nineveh. The men were used as forced labour in the limestone quarries.

THE KING'S MEN
A king was constantly surrounded by bodyguards, astrologers and other members of the court including provincial governors who helped him run the empire. His attendants included scribes to write down his orders, messengers to deliver them and an attendant to hold a parasol and shield him from the sun. King Ashurnasirpal is celebrating a successful bull hunt with priests and musicians.

MAKE A PARASOL

You will need: pencil, coloured card 60cm x 60cm, scissors, masking tape, paints in bright colours and paintbrushes, white card, string or twine, glue, dowel.

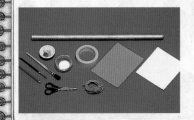

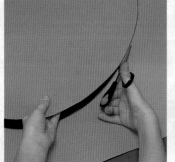

1 Draw a circle on the coloured card measuring roughly 60cm across. Cut out the circle with the scissors keeping the edge as neat as possible.

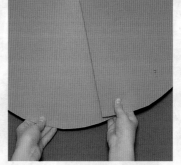

2 Cut a slit from the edge of the circle to the centre. Pull one edge of the slit over the other to make a conical shape. Secure with masking tape.

3 Paint your parasol with red paint. Leave to dry. Then paint stripes in lots of different shades of orange and red from the top to the bottom.

TOWARDS A NEW LIFE

Defeated people camp out en route to a new life in Assyria. The Assyrian Empire grew so big, that it could take months to travel back from a newly conquered territory. People were usually kept together in families and given homes in the countryside. Often they were set to work to cultivate more land.

KEEPING ACCOUNTS

Assyrian scribes at the governor's palace at Til Barsip on the River Euphrates make a note of taxes demanded by the king. Taxes were exacted not only from the local Assyrian people, but also from the conquered territories. They could be paid in produce, such as grain, horses or cattle, and wine.

Kings were accompanied by an attendant carrying a sunshade, which was probably made of fine woollen material and decorated with tassels.

USEFUL TRIBUTE

Horses are given as tributes to the Assyrian king from a conquered people. They will be used to swell the chariot and cavalry units in the Assyrian army. The best-bred and strongest horses came from the foothills of the Zagros Mountains to the east of Assyria. The king also demanded food for the horses.

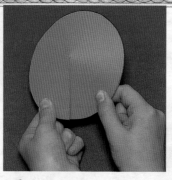

4 Cut 20 oval shapes about 5cm by 4cm from the white card. Cover with a base colour of gold. Leave to dry, then paint with bright designs.

5 Use the scissors to make holes around the edge of the parasol and in the ovals. Attach the ovals to the parasol with twine, knotting it as shown.

6 Cut a small circle out of coloured card measuring 10cm across. Make a slit to the centre, and pull one edge over the other as before. Paint the small cone gold.

7 Glue it to the top of the parasol. Paint the handle with gold paint and allow to dry. Attach it to the inside of the parasol using plenty of masking tape.

Fighting Forces

THE EARLIEST HISTORICAL RECORDS of Mesopotamia tell of city-states at war with one another. These were usually local disputes over pieces of land or the ownership of canals. Later, when powerful kings created empires, they went to war with foreign countries. King Sargon of Agade, for example, subdued all the cities of Sumer and then went on to conquer the great cities of Mari on the River Euphrates and Ebla in northern Syria. Assyria and Babylonia were often at war in the first millennium BC. The walls of Assyrian palaces are decorated with reliefs showing frightened groups of Babylonians hiding among the reeds of the marshes, as well as the conquest of Elam, Judah and Phoenician cities.

WHEELED ADVANTAGE
An Assyrian king charges along in his chariot at a lion hunt. Chariots were also used to ride into battle. The Assyrians perfected the art of chariot warfare, which gave them a big advantage over enemies who were fighting on foot.

IN THE BEGINNING
A model of a very early chariot, about 4,000 years old, shows the first wheel designs of solid wood. By the time of the Assyrian Empire, about 900-600 BC, war chariots had spoked wooden wheels with metal rims.

THE KING'S GUARDS
A panel from the palace of the Persian kings at Susa shows a long procession of king's guards. The guards are armed with spears, and carry quivers full of arrows. King Cyrus of Persia conquered Babylon in 539BC.

MAKE A CHARIOT
You will need: pen, cardboard, scissors, paints and paintbrushes, flour, water and newspaper to make papier mâché, glue, masking tape, 2 x dowel 16cm long, card tubes, needle, 4 cocktail sticks.

1 Cut four circles about 7cm in width out of the card. Use the scissors to make a hole in the centre of each circle. Enlarge the holes with a pen.

2 Cut out two sides for the chariot 12cm long x 8cm high as shown, one back 9 x 8cm, one front 9 x 15cm, one top 9 x 7cm and one base 12 x 9cm.

3 Trim the top of the front to two curves as shown. Stick the side pieces to the front and back using masking tape. Stick on the base and top.

SLINGS AND ARROWS
Assyrian foot-soldiers used rope slings and stone balls the size of modern tennis-balls. Others fired arrows while sheltering behind tall wicker shields. They wore helmets of bronze or iron and were protected by metal scale armour and leather boots.

GOING INTO BATTLE
Sumerian chariot drivers charge into battle. A soldier armed with spears stands on the footplate of each chariot ready to jump off and fight. They are all protected by thick leather cloaks and helmets. The chariots were drawn by onegars (wild asses).

STORMING A CITY
Many Assyrian fighting methods can be seen in the palace reliefs at the city of Nimrud. In this scene, the Assyrians storm an enemy city which stands on a hill. A siege engine with spears projecting from the front breaks down the walls. Attacking soldiers would also scale the walls with the help of siege ladders, protected by archers.

Your chariot copies a clay model made in northern Mesopotamia over 4,000 years ago.

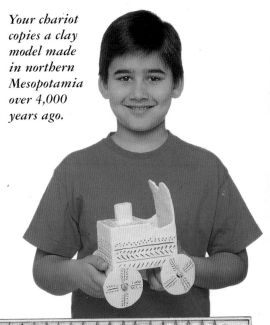

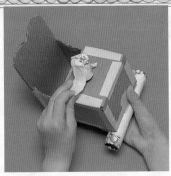

4 Roll up a piece of newspaper to make a cylinder shape 3cm long, and attach it to the chariot. Attach the cardboard tubes to the bottom of the chariot.

5 Mix a paste of flour and water. Dip newspaper strips into the paste to make papier mâché. Cover the chariot with layers of papier mâché. Leave to dry.

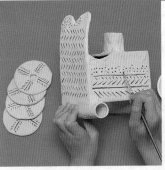

6 Paint the whole chariot cream. Add detail using brown paint. Paint the wheels, too. Make a hole with the needle in each end of the dowels.

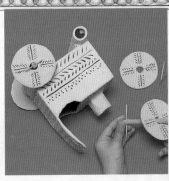

7 Insert a cocktail stick in the dowel, add a wheel and insert into the tube. Fix another wheel and stick to the other end. Repeat with the other wheels.

Palace Builders

Mesopotamian palace was not just built as the king's residence but also as a centre of government. Many were impressive buildings where the kings received ambassadors.

Most information about palace buildings comes from the Assyrian palaces at Nimrud, Nineveh and Khorsabad. King Ashurnasirpal built a magnificent palace at Nimrud on the River Tigris in the 900s BC. He knocked down the old city and built a huge platform of 120 layers of mud-bricks as a foundation. On that platform, he wrote, 'I built my palace with seven beautiful halls roofed with boxwood, cedar, cypress and terebinth wood. I decorated the doors with bands of bronze. I carved and painted the walls with vivid paint showing my victories.' The king had lapis lazuli coloured glazed bricks specially made and set them in the walls above the gates.

HAULING WOOD
Workers drag heavy pieces of cedar wood to the building site of the palace at Nimrud. The timber for the palace roof and the imposing doors at the entrance was imported from Lebanon, which was famous for its pine and cedar wood. It came by boat along the Mediterranean coast. Once the ships were unloaded, the timber was hauled overland to the city.

MIGHTY BEASTS
Lamassus were huge statues that stood at palace entrances to frighten evil spirits away from the palace and the king. They were carved from a single block of gypsum, a soft stone that was easy to carve, and weighed several tonnes. They have five limbs so that they have four legs when seen from the side. The extra leg was so that they did not appear one-legged if seen from the front.

EXOTIC SETTING
Assyrian palaces were often set in exotic gardens. At Nimrud in 970BC, King Ashurnasirpal took pride in his garden where he planted all kinds of seeds and plants brought back from his campaigns in foreign countries. He had vines, nut trees and fruit trees. He wrote: 'Pomegranates glow in my garden of happiness like stars in the sky. In my garden the plants vie with each other in fragrance. The paths are well kept and there are canals so the plants can be watered.'

YOU HAVE BEEN WARNED

Palace walls were decorated with carved reliefs designed to impress visitors, and to show that the king was fulfilling the role given to him by the gods. In this relief at Ashurnasirpal's palace at Nimrud, the king is depicted heroically fighting a snarling lion, proving that he is the protector of his people. Other scenes showed the king victorious in battle, as a warning to anyone considering rebellion against Assyria.

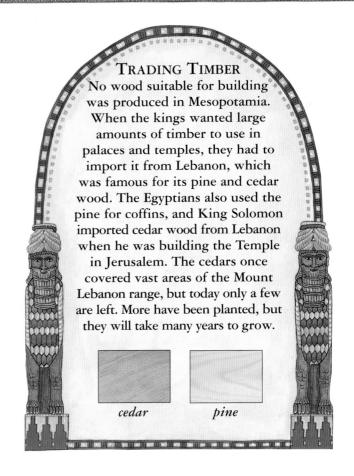

TRADING TIMBER

No wood suitable for building was produced in Mesopotamia. When the kings wanted large amounts of timber to use in palaces and temples, they had to import it from Lebanon, which was famous for its pine and cedar wood. The Egyptians also used the pine for coffins, and King Solomon imported cedar wood from Lebanon when he was building the Temple in Jerusalem. The cedars once covered vast areas of the Mount Lebanon range, but today only a few are left. More have been planted, but they will take many years to grow.

cedar *pine*

WEALTH AND SPLENDOUR

Henry Layard, the archaeologist who excavated the city of Nimrud in the 1840s, imagined the city looked like this at the height of its powers. His picture was based on his excavations, but it may not be entirely accurate. However, it gives an idea of the splendour and wealth of an Assyrian capital city. Archaeologists found the remains of several palaces and temples at Nimrud. They had been built by various kings in the 8th and 9th centuries BC.

Furnishing the Palace

WOMAN IN A WINDOW
The Phoenicians were very skilful at ivory carving. This piece, showing a woman looking out of a window, is typical of their work. The holes were used to attach it to a mirror handle.

THE ASSYRIAN KINGS loved the luxury of ivory furniture. They filled their palaces with ivory beds, armchairs, footstools and tables. No complete pieces of ivory furniture have survived to modern times, but Henry Layard found part of an ivory throne at Nimrud in the 1840s. He also found some whole tusks of elephant ivory and a great many small, carved ivory plaques that were once attached to the wooden framework of pieces of furniture. The Assyrians were free to use as much ivory as they liked because elephants were not then an endangered species. No textiles have survived but palaces would probably have been made more comfortable with cushions and woollen rugs. Stone entrances to the palace rooms carved in the form of floral-patterned carpets show us what the rugs may have looked like.

INSIDE THE PALACE
Palaces were built from mud-brick, but the lower interior walls were decorated with carved and painted slabs of stone. Teams of sculptors and artists produced scenes showing the king's military campaigns and wild bull and lion hunts. The upper walls were plastered and painted with similar scenes to glorify the king and impress foreign visitors. Paints were ground from minerals. Red and brown paints were made from ochres, blues and greens from copper ores, azurite and malachite.

MAKE A BRONZE AND IVORY MIRROR

You will need: pencil, strong white and reflective card, ruler, scissors, thick dowel, masking tape, flour, water and newspaper for papier mâché, sandpaper, paints and brushes, glue.

1 Using a pencil, draw a circle 12cm across on to the strong white card. Add a handle about 6cm long and 2.5cm wide as shown. Cut out.

2 Take a length of dowel about 20cm long. Fix the dowel to the handle using masking tape. Bend the card round the dowel as shown in the picture.

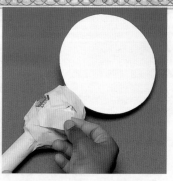

3 Scrunch up a piece of newspaper into a ball. Attach the newspaper ball to the top of the handle with masking tape as shown.

LUXURY IN THE GARDEN

King Ashurbanipal and his wife even had luxurious ivory furniture in the palace gardens at Nineveh. In this picture, the king is reclining on an elaborate ivory couch decorated with tiny carved and gilded lions. The queen is sitting on an ivory chair with a high back and resting her feet on a footstool. Cushions make the furniture more comfortable. Ivory workers used drills and chisels similar to those used by carpenters. The ivory plaques had signs on them to show how they should be slotted together.

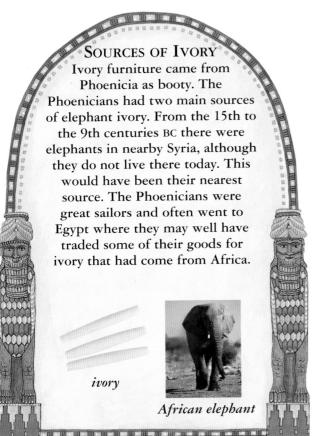

SOURCES OF IVORY

Ivory furniture came from Phoenicia as booty. The Phoenicians had two main sources of elephant ivory. From the 15th to the 9th centuries BC there were elephants in nearby Syria, although they do not live there today. This would have been their nearest source. The Phoenicians were great sailors and often went to Egypt where they may well have traded some of their goods for ivory that had come from Africa.

ivory

African elephant

Polished bronze was used for mirrors in ancient times. A mirror with a carved ivory handle would have belonged to a wealthy woman.

BOY-EATER

This furniture plaque shows a boy being eaten by a lioness. The boy's kilt is covered with gold leaf, and his curly hair is made of tiny gold pins. There are lotus flowers and papyrus plants in the background, inlaid with real lapis lazuli and carnelian. Sometimes ivory was stained or inlaid with paste to imitate jewels.

4 Make a paste with flour and water, and dip strips of newspaper in it. Cover the handle with several layers, allowing each layer to dry.

5 Use newspaper to make the nose and ears. Add a strip of papier mâché at the top of the head for the crown. Leave to dry, then sandpaper until smooth.

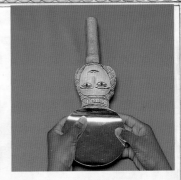

6 Paint a base coat of grey paint on the face and bronze on the handle. Then add the details of the face and crown in black using a fine paintbrush.

7 Cut out a circle of reflective card to match the mirror shape. Glue the reflective card carefully on to the white card. This is your bronze mirror.

Marvellous Sculptures

FROM THE BEGINNING of the civilization in Mesopotamia, sculpture was an important art. The earliest sculptors were good at making small statues and figurines. Some were made of stone, but others were of painted clay. Apart from boulders found in rivers there was no stone in Sumer, so most of the materials for sculpture had to be imported. In Assyria, further north, there were quarries near the modern town of Mosul, where a kind of gypsum was found. This is a fairly soft stone which can be carved in great detail. Large pieces of gypsum were cut with pickaxes and sawn with two-handled saws. The slabs were then put on carts and taken to the river where they were transferred on to rafts and floated to the building site. The slabs were carved and painted after they were placed in position.

PROTECTIVE GENIE
Many rooms in the palace King Ashurnasirpal built at Nimrud in the 900s BC were decorated with genies. These creatures have human bodies but the wings, heads and beaks of birds of prey. They were carved to protect the king and the courtiers from evil spirits. The genie shown here is carrying a cone and a bucket and seems to be using them for some kind of ritual. He was possibly blessing the king.

OFF TO WORK
Men go to work at a gypsum quarry near to the modern city of Mosul on the River Tigris. It was not far from the ancient Assyrian cities of Nimrud and Nineveh. The workers are carrying pickaxes to hack out massive blocks of stone. The two-handled saws will be used to slice the blocks into thinner slabs to be fixed to the walls of a palace before they are carved and painted by teams of artists.

GLAZED BRICKS FROM BABYLON
Babylonian kings decorated their city with beautiful sculptures made of glazed bricks. This panel comes from the Ishtar Gate at Babylon. It shows the mushushshu (snake dragon) of the city god Marduk. The gate also featured bulls. The animals were made from glazed bricks formed in special moulds so that they stood out from the wall as if they had been carved.

CHOSEN BY ASHUR

In this carved relief from the throne room in Ashurnasirpal's palace, the king is shown twice. He is standing in front of a sacred tree. Above the tree is a winged disc containing the figure of a god. He seems to be pointing at Ashurnasirpal to indicate he is the god's choice. The god could be Ashur.

MONSTER GUARDIAN

Assyrian palace entrances were guarded by lamassus, immense statues three metres high or more. When a sculpture was complete, it was painted to make it more lifelike. Lamassus were strange monsters with the bodies of lions or bulls, the wings of mighty birds, human heads and caps with horns to show they had divine powers. They combined all the most powerful forces of heaven and earth and were supposed to prowl up and down warding off evil spirits from the palaces. They are symbols of pent-up supernatural fury.

PUBLIC DISPLAY

Assyrian kings liked to be seen as faithful servants of the gods. They often ordered a stela (stone slab) to be set up in a public place and carved with pictures. This stela was set up outside the temple of Ninurta, the war god, at Nimrud. It shows King Ashurnasirpal showing respect to the gods. The symbols represent different gods – the goddess Ishtar (star), Adad the storm god (forked lightning), Sin the moon god (crescent Moon), Shamash the sun god (disc with flames), and Ashur (horned cap).

RELIEF WORK

Stone was cut into large slabs on the quarry site using tough, two-handled saws. The slabs were taken to the palace or temple. Workers joined them together by hammering lead dowels and clamps into them with mallets. Teams of sculptors would then carve the figures in outline with big bronze or iron chisels. They would use finer ones for details of face, hair, jewellery and dress. The carved surface was polished with sand or painted.

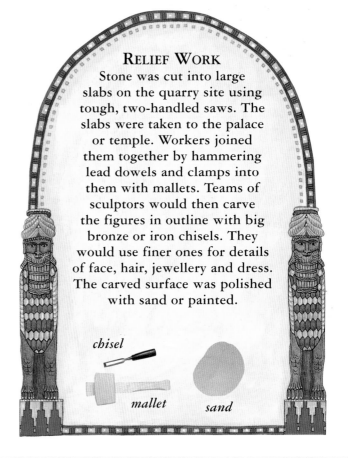

chisel

mallet   *sand*

The Lion Hunt of the King

FROM EARLIEST TIMES, Mesopotamian kings hunted lions, because lions represented evil and it was the duty of the king to protect his people. The first known picture of a king doing this is on a stela (stone slab) from the ancient Sumerian city of Uruk and is over 5,000 years old. Most of our information about royal lion hunts comes from reliefs in a sloping corridor of the palace of the Assyrian king Ashurbanipal (669-631BC) at Nineveh, which show every stage of a hunt. When the lion had been killed, the king poured a libation of oil or wine over the body, and offered it to the gods.

AFRICAN LION
Mesopotamian mountain lions were smaller than the African lion shown here but were just as dangerous. They came from the mountains and attacked the villagers of the plain and their farm animals. The mountain lions are extinct now but lived in Mesopotamia until the 1800s.

LION ARENA
A hungry snarling lion has been released from its cage. The kings did not hunt lions in open country but in special arenas heavily guarded by soldiers, gamekeepers and fierce dogs. The royal hunting ground was just outside Nineveh, and lions were brought there in strong cages. Local people sometimes climbed nearby hills to get a good view.

HUNTING FOR FOOD
The Mesopotamians were good farmers, growing barley and other crops and raising sheep and goats, but they also had to go hunting for meat to supplement their diet. These men have shot a deer using a bow and arrow and trapped a rabbit in a snare. Sometimes, they caught birds using nets, and they collected locusts. Marsh scenes carved on the palace walls show men and boys fishing from boats or sitting on inflated animal skins.

MAKE A ROYAL TUNIC
You will need: coloured cotton fabric 90cm by 230cm, white pencil, tape measure, scissors, pins, needle and thread, white cotton fabric 50cm by 24cm, pencil, fabric paints and paintbrushes, glue, sponge.

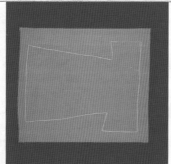

1 Fold the coloured cloth in two. Using the white pencil, draw a tunic shape as shown. It should be roughly 90 cm across and 115 cm long.

2 Cut out the tunic shape, making sure that you are cutting through both layers of material. Be careful to cut the lines as smoothly as you can.

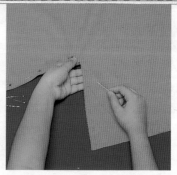

3 Pin around the edges of the two tunic shapes. Then sew down the sides and across the top, making sure you leave holes for your head and arms.

PROTECTOR OF THE PEOPLE

Hunters were heavily armed. Here King Ashurbanipal's arrows have only injured the lion. When the lion attacks his horse, the king plunges his spear into it. Eventually, the lion is worn out, and the king dismounts and runs it through with his sword. The king is not just hunting for sport, but because the lion symbolized evil to the Mesopotamians. It is the king's religious duty to protect his people from such evil.

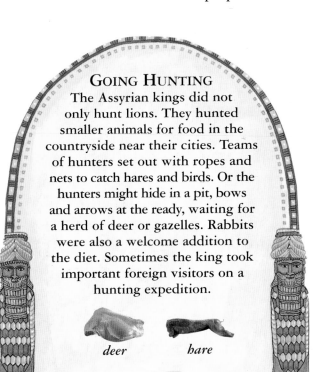

GOING HUNTING

The Assyrian kings did not only hunt lions. They hunted smaller animals for food in the countryside near their cities. Teams of hunters set out with ropes and nets to catch hares and birds. Or the hunters might hide in a pit, bows and arrows at the ready, waiting for a herd of deer or gazelles. Rabbits were also a welcome addition to the diet. Sometimes the king took important foreign visitors on a hunting expedition.

deer   hare

rabbit

Royal robes were made from fine woollen material. Patterns were woven into the fabric or embroidered later. The most highly prized cloth was imported from the Phoenician cities, where it was coloured purple with dye from murex shellfish.

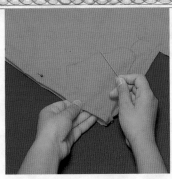

4 Neaten the edges of the arms and around the bottom by turning in a small amount of material to make a hem. Pin the hem, then sew it as shown.

5 Draw strips about 3cm wide on the white material. Paint brightly coloured decorative designs along the strips with the fabric paints.

6 When the paint is dry, cut out the decorative strips, keeping the lines as straight as you can. Glue the strips on to the tunic across the chest and arms.

7 Use the sponge to make decorative patterns on the rest of the tunic. Dip the sponge into fabric paint and press it lightly on to the fabric.

Kingship

THE KINGS OF MESOPOTAMIA considered themselves to have been chosen by the gods. For example, Ur-Nanshe of Lagash (2480BC) said that he was granted kingship by Enlil, chief of the gods, and Ashurbanipal (669BC) claimed he was the son of the Assyrian god, Ashur, and his wife, Belit. The Mesopotamian kings ran the state on the god's behalf. Even in the Assyrian Empire, when the kings had grand titles such as 'King of the Universe', they still felt they were responsible to the gods for the well-being of their people. Another of their titles was 'Shepherd'. This meant they had to look after their people, just as a shepherd tends his flock.

AUTHORITY
This onyx mace belonged to the Babylonian kings. It was a symbol of authority. At the New Year festival, the king placed his mace before the statue of the chief god, Marduk. He was later given back the mace so that he could reign for another year.

SUN GOD TABLET FROM SIPPAR
Kings had to see that temples and statues of the gods were kept in good repair. This tablet shows King Nabu-apla-iddina of Babylon being led into the presence of the god Shamash. The story on the tablet tells us that the king wanted to make a new statue of the god. He was meant to repair the old one but it had been stolen by enemies. Fortunately a priest found a model of the statue that could be copied.

MAKE A FLY WHISK
You will need: calico fabric, pencil, ruler, PVA glue and brush, scissors, thick card, paints and paintbrushes, newspaper.

1 Draw long leaf shapes about 45cm long on to the calico fabric with the pencil. Paint the shapes with watered down PVA glue. Leave to dry.

2 Cut out the leaf shapes. Make a card spine for the centre of each leaf as shown, thicker at the bottom than at the top, and glue them on.

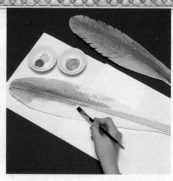

3 Paint the leaves in gold, yellow and red paints on both sides. Add fine detail by cutting into the edge of each leaf using the scissors.

FIGHTING FOR THE GODS

Kings believed that they were commanded by the gods to conquer in their name. In this relief, King Sennacherib is sitting on his throne receiving the booty and prisoners taken after the city of Lachish had fallen. The king devoted a whole room in his palace at Nineveh to the story of this siege. He also made war on Babylon and completely devastated the city. In 612BC the Babylonians had their revenge. They destroyed Nineveh and hacked out Sennacherib's face on this sculpture.

EXPLORATION AND DISCOVERY

Another mark of good kingship was the expansion of knowledge. King Shalmaneser III sent an expedition to find the source of the river Tigris pictured here. When his men found it, they set up a stela to record the event and made offerings to the gods to celebrate. Many of the Mesopotamian kings were learned men. Kings such as Ashurbanipal collected clay tablets to make great libraries. Others collected exotic plants and animals.

Fly whisks made of long thin leaves or feathery reeds kept the flies away from the king. They could also be used as a fan to keep him cool.

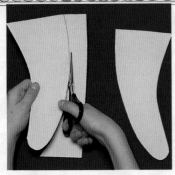

4 Draw two identical handle shapes on to the stiff card. They should be about 22cm long and 10cm wide at the top. Cut out the shapes with the scissors.

5 Tear up newspaper strips and dip into glue. Wrap the strips around the edges of the two handles to fasten them together. Leave the top of the handle unglued.

6 Decorate the handle with gold paint. Leave to dry. Paint decorative details on to the gold with black paint using a fine paintbrush.

7 Glue the bottoms of the leaves and push them into the top of the handle, between the two pieces of cardboard. Spread the leaves well apart.

Royal Libraries and Museums

WHAT THE FUTURE HOLDS
Clay models of sheep's livers were used for divining what the future might hold. They were divided into zones with names such as Station, Path, Finger and Palace Gates. The diviners used these to interpret what they saw in the livers of sacrificed animals. If the Palace Gates were open, for example, this could mean attack by an enemy, or famine. If they were together, it was a good sign.

IN THE MID-700s BC, King Ashurbanipal decided to found a great library at Nineveh. Every temple in the land had a library, so he sent his scribes round all the temples of Babylonia with instructions to bring him anything that looked interesting. If the priests were reluctant to let a tablet go, the scribes were told to make a copy. The library at Nineveh eventually contained over 25,000 clay tablets, and most of what is known about Mesopotamian learning comes from there.

In the Nineveh library were ancient myths and legends such as the *Epic of Gilgamesh* and the *Birth Legend of Sargon of Agade*, dictionaries, mathematical problems, and texts on astronomy, astrology and medicine. There were collections of clay models of sheep's livers and lists of weather omens for predicting future events. For example, if it was foggy in a particular month, the land was expected to go to ruin.

The Babylonian king, Nebuchadnezzar II, founded a museum, which had statues, a stela of a Mari governor who introduced bee-keeping into Mesopotamia, and objects and clay tablets that went back to Sumerian times.

WRITING TO GODS
If a king wanted to build a temple or go on a campaign, he asked the gods about it first. The Assyrian king, Esarhaddon, wrote letters to the sun god, Shamash, which were kept in the library at Nineveh. He wrote a question on a clay tablet and asked for a clear answer. The tablet was then placed in front of the god's statue. An animal was slaughtered and the liver examined. The diviners (fortune-tellers) could tell by looking at it whether or not the god approved.

WORK IT OUT
King Ashurbanipal, founder of the library at Nineveh, collected many mathematical tablets. The Babylonians were the world's first mathematicians, and worked out many processes that are still used today. The library had a number of mathematical tables that made it easier for people to divide and multiply numbers. Clay tablets included tables showing reciprocals, square numbers and square roots.

DISCOVERY

Before the discovery of the 4,000-year-old library at Ebla, no one knew that libraries existed at such an early date. The city was mentioned in Sumerian texts but its location was not known. The mound at Tell Mardik in northern Syria was first excavated in the 1960s by Italian archaeologists. Proof that it was the ancient city of Ebla came with the discovery of the royal library, and a royal statue inscribed with the words 'Ibbit-Lim, King of Ebla.'

LOOK IT UP

The oldest library found in the world so far dates from the 3rd millennium BC and was discovered at Ebla in north Syria. The city lay beyond Mesopotamia, but the people used similar writing, and kept records just like the Sumerians. This library was found in the palace at Ebla. Tablets were in heaps on the floor, but the excavators could see marks on the walls where shelves had once been. Librarians kept all the tablets about a particular subject together on one part of the shelves. Small tablets were stored in baskets.

MAP OF THE WORLD

A unique map of the world was found in the library of Ashurbanipal at Nineveh, although it was originally drawn up in Babylon. It shows the world as the Babylonians saw it. The earth is a flat disc surrounded by ocean. Babylon is named in the box inside the circle. The river Euphrates flows through the middle. Mysterious regions lie to the north, south, east and west. The north is described as 'the land where the Sun is never seen'. Few people had ever been there, but the text says Sargon of Agade had. He is known from his own records to have conquered distant regions, and was still regarded as a hero hundreds of years later.

Maths, Medicine and Astronomy

THE MESOPOTAMIANS liked working things out. They had two number systems, one using 10 as a base and the other, 60. The Sumerians were the first to calculate time in hour-long units of 60 minutes, and their astronomers worked out a calendar based on 12- and 28-day cycles and 7-day weeks from studying the moon and the seasons. In particular, the Babylonians were especially interested in studying the heavens, and their astronomers could predict events such as eclipses, solstices and equinoxes.

Mesopotamian doctors did not really understand how the body works, but made lists of patients' symptoms. Their observations were passed on to the Greeks hundreds of years later and so became one of the foundations of modern medicine.

HEAVY COUGH CURE
This tablet suggests mixing balsam (a herb) with strong beer, honey and oil to cure a cough. The mixture was taken hot, without food. Then the patient's throat was tickled with a feather to make him sick. Other prescriptions used mice, dogs' tails and urine.

BAD OMEN
Eclipses were considered a bad sign. However, an eclipse that was obscured by cloud did not count. When an eclipse could not be seen in a royal city, the king was told it had nothing to do with him or his country and he should not worry about it.

MEDICINAL BREW
Servants are distilling essence of cedar, a vital ingredient for a headache cure. Cedar twigs were put into a pot, and heated to give off a vapour. It condensed against the cooler lid and trickled into the rim of the pot from where it was collected. The essence was mixed with honey, resin from pine, myrrh and spruce trees, and fat from a sheep's kidney.

MAKE A SET OF LION WEIGHTS

You will need: pebbles of various sizes, kitchen scales, modelling clay, cutting board, cocktail stick, paints and paintbrushes.

1 Weigh a pebble and add modelling clay to make it up to a weight of 225g. Once the clay has dried out, the final weight will be only about 200g.

2 Take a portion of the weighed modelling clay and shape it into a rectangle roughly 12cm by 7cm. This will be the base for your weight.

3 Wrap another piece of the weighed modelling clay around the weighed pebble to make the lion's body. Shape the body into a pear shape.

SKY MAP

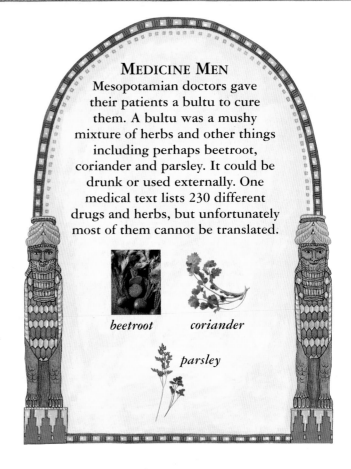

The sky in this sky map is divided into eight parts and the stars in each section are indicated. The heavens were seen as a source of information about the future, so the kings often consulted astronomers. One astronomer wrote to the king in the 600s BC: 'I am always looking at the sky but nothing unusual has appeared above the horizon'.

MEDICINE MEN

Mesopotamian doctors gave their patients a bultu to cure them. A bultu was a mushy mixture of herbs and other things including perhaps beetroot, coriander and parsley. It could be drunk or used externally. One medical text lists 230 different drugs and herbs, but unfortunately most of them cannot be translated.

beetroot   *coriander*

parsley

WEIGHTS AND MEASURES

Officials weigh metal objects that have been taken as booty after a victory. The duck-shaped object is a weight. The kings were responsible for seeing that weights and measures were exact and that nobody cheated customers. Prices were fixed by law and calculated in shekels (1 shekel was about 8g of silver).

Bronze lion weights from a set belonging to King Shalmaneser V have been found at Nimrud. Like your weights they were of different sizes.

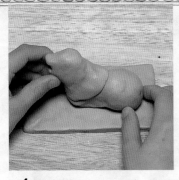 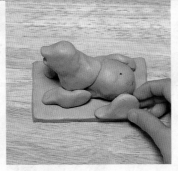  

4 Position the pebble and clay on to its base. Add another piece of weighed clay to form the head and mane. Shape the face and jaw with your fingers.

5 Model four pieces of weighed clay to make the lion's four legs and stick them on to the body. Flatten the clay slightly at each end for the paws.

6 Make a tail and ears using up the remaining weighed clay. Using the cocktail stick, add extra detail to the face, mane, paws and tail. Leave to dry.

7 Paint the lion and the base cream. Flick with brown paint for a mottled appearance. Add details to the face, mane and paws. Make more lions for a set.

Babylonian Power

ATTACK ON BABYLON
Assyrian kings usually showed great respect for Marduk, the god of Babylon. But when the Babylonians allowed King Sennacherib's son to be captured, the angry king attacked Babylon and burnt down Marduk's temple. His son and grandson were so worried by this that they decided to rebuild the city and temple as quickly as they could. This stela shows Sennacherib's grandson Ashurbanipal holding a brick-basket for building.

REBUILDING BABYLON
Nabopolassar and his son, Nebuchadnezzar built a new city worthy of Babylon's status as a world power in the 500s BC. The city was constructed on both banks of the River Euphrates with a bridge on stone pillars connecting the two parts of the new Babylon. There were several temples and palaces. A massive 8-km wall surrounded the city. The road on top of the wall was so wide that two four-horse chariots could pass each other.

THE NAME BABYLON means Gateway of the Gods. Although Babylon was quite a small place in Sumerian times, it began to grow in importance from the time of King Hammurabi. It soon became the chief city of the whole of southern Mesopotamia, and this region became known as Babylonia. The main temple of the god Marduk was in Babylon, and the city became a great centre of learning. Many of the texts in King Ashurbanipal's library came from Babylonia, or were copies of Babylonian works. Towards the end of the 600s BC, the Babylonians attacked and destroyed the Assyrian cities of Ashur, Nimrud and Nineveh. The Assyrian Empire came to an end, and for a time Babylon became very powerful under its great king, Nebuchadnezzar II. King Nebuchadnezzar took over many parts of the ancient world that had once belonged to Assyria, including Palestine and Phoenicia. When King Necho of Egypt challenged Nebuchadnezzar and tried to take some of the old Assyrian territory for himself, the Babylonian king promptly chased him back to his country.

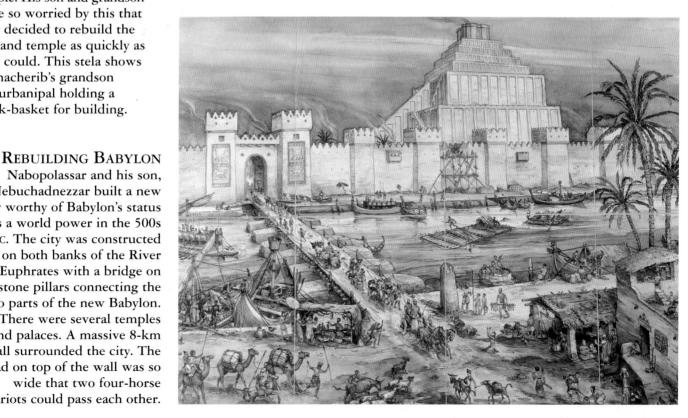

GATEWAY TO THE GODDESS

The inner wall of the city of Babylon had several gateways leading into the city, each having the name of an important god or goddess. The most splendid was the Ishtar Gate, named after the goddess of love and war and built in the reign of Nebuchadnezzar II. The gate was decorated with blue-glazed bricks inset with three-dimensional sculptures of moulded bricks. These showed the bull of Adad and the snake dragon of Marduk, the god of Babylon.

A FORMIDABLE ENEMY

King Marduk-apla-iddina was the very first Babylonian king to be mentioned by name in the Bible, where he is called Merodach Baladan. This boundary stone was found in Babylon and shows him making a grant of land to the governor of Babylon in around 700 BC. Marduk-apla-iddina fought many battles against the Assyrian kings, Sargon and Sennacherib. Even after he had been defeated and forced to retreat to the marshes, he continued to stir up trouble for the Assyrians.

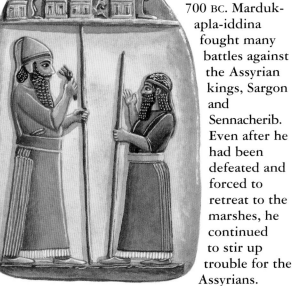

THE WAY OF THE LION

Babylon had a special road for processions. The Processional Way led from the temple of Marduk through the Ishtar Gate on its way out of the city to the temple where the New Year festival was held. The way was decorated with blue-glazed tiles and moulded brick figures of lions. Each year the statues of the gods were carried along here to attend a special ceremony in which the Babylonian Story of Creation was enacted and the king was re-invested with royal power.

WONDER OF THE WORLD

The city of Babylon was famous for its Hanging Gardens. Like the pyramids at Giza in ancient Egypt, they were one of the Seven Wonders of the Ancient World. Tradition says the magnificent gardens were created by one of its kings. He had married a Persian wife who was homesick for the hills of her own country. The king loved her so much he built an artificial mountain and planted it with trees and flowers. Later many people tried to find the gardens but no one has ever succeeded, although strangely one modern scholar thinks they were in Nineveh rather than Babylon.

Bible Links

FLOODS
A tale like the Bible story of Noah's Ark was found in the library at Nineveh. King Utnapishtim was warned that the god Enlil was going to send a flood and told to make a boat and take his family, all the animals and craftworkers on board. It rained for seven days and seven nights. When it stopped, the king sent out birds to see if the water had gone down. The goddess Ishtar put her necklace in the sky as a sign this would never happen again.

THERE ARE MANY LINKS between Mesopotamia and the Bible. Mesopotamian flood stories are remarkably like the story of Noah's Ark. Abraham, the father of the Israelite and Arab nations, lived at the Sumerian city of Ur before he and his family set off for the Promised Land. Several of the laws and customs relating to marriage and adoption mentioned in these stories about Abraham are like those of Mesopotamia. Jonah was instructed by God to go to the Assyrian city of Nineveh, and the Jewish people were exiled from their Promised Land to Babylon. Assyrian records often include kings and events mentioned in the Old Testament.

One Assyrian king, Shalmaneser III, records his victory at the Battle of Qarqar in Syria. He says he fought against twelve kings, one of whom was Ahab of Israel. This is the first time a king of Israel appears in the history of another country. From this time onward, the paths of Assyria and Israel often crossed.

DESERT JOURNEY
Abraham, the father of the Jewish and Arab nations, travels from the Sumerian city of Ur to the country God has promised his people. In this painting of the 1800s, Abraham is leading a wandering existence in a desert landscape with his flock of sheep moving from one area to another in search of grazing ground for his animals. However, people would not have used camels at the time he is thought to have lived, about 2000BC. Camels were not used for transport in Mesopotamia until about 1000BC.

BLACK OBELISK

The man bowing in front of the Assyrian king, Shalmaneser III, could be Jehu, King of Israel. Israel had been an enemy of Assyria, but Jehu has decided to change sides and become an ally of Assyria. The picture appears on the Black Obelisk, which tells of Shalmaneser III's conquests at war. The writing says that the gifts of the Israelite king are being presented to show his loyalty and win Shalmaneser's approval.

WAR CORRESPONDENTS

The Bible reports that the Assyrian king Sennacherib laid siege to Jerusalem when Hezekiah was king of Judah. It says he withdrew from the siege when an angel attacked his army. In Sennacherib's version of events on this clay prism (a hollow tablet), he does not say he was defeated or that he captured Jerusalem. All he says is he shut Hezekiah up like a bird in a cage.

EXILE IN BABYLON

The great Babylonian king of the 500s BC was Nebuchadnezzar II, who took over many parts of the ancient world that had formerly been part of the Assyrian Empire. In 597BC he attacked Jerusalem, the chief city of the kingdom of Judah, a scene imagined here by a medieval painter. At the end of a successful siege, he took the king, his courtiers, the army and all the craftworkers to Babylon. There they spent many years far from home, a time known among Jewish people as the Exile. Nebuchadnezzar took treasures from the temple in Jerusalem as booty. He appointed another king, Zedekiah, to rule in Jerusalem. Nebuchadnezzar returned some years later when Zedekiah rebelled, and punished him severely.

GLOSSARY

A

agriculture Farming, especially the cultivation of crops.

alabaster A gleaming white stone, a type of gypsum.

amethyst A purple crystal, a type of quartz.

amulet A lucky charm.

archaeologist Someone who studies ancient remains, such as ruins, tombs, seeds, tools or coins, in order to learn about the past.

artefact An object that has been made by a person, such as a pot, a textile or a coin.

astrology The study of the position and movement of the stars and planets in order to foretell the future.

astronomy The scientific study of the stars and planets.

B

booty Valuable things seized and carried off by a victorious army.

C

campaign A series of battles fought by a ruler to bring an area under his control.

canopic jar A pottery jar used to hold the lungs, liver, intestines and stomach of a dead person.

cast To shape molten metal by pouring it into a mould, where it hardens.

▲ *Marduk, the god of Babylon.*

cataract Waterfall or white-water rapids.

chariot A horse-drawn cart, used for warfare, hunting or racing.

city-state A small independent state, based upon a single city and its surrounding villages and countryside.

civil servant Someone who works as a government adminstrator.

civilization A society that makes advances in arts, sciences, technology, law or government.

conscript Someone who is called up by the government to serve in the army.

cosmetics Powder, paint or ointments designed to make someone more attractive; make-up.

crook and flail A hooked stick and a jointed stick, sacred to the god Osiris. The pharaohs carried the crook and flail as symbols of royal authority.

cubit A unit of measurement, the length of a forearm.

cuneiform Wedge-shaped. The name given to the script invented by the Sumerians and also used by the Babylonians and Assyrians.

D

decipher To work out the meaning of signs and symbols.

deity A god or goddess.

delta A coastal region where a river splits into separate waterways before flowing into the sea.

demotic A simplified script used in the later periods of ancient Egypt.

diviner Someone who foretells the future, for example by examining animals' livers or the pattern oil makes on water.

◄ *Assyrian royal hunt.*

drought A long, dry period without rainfall.

dynasty A royal family, or the period it remains in power.

E

embalm To preserve a dead body.

empire A number of different lands coming under the rule of a single government.

epic A long poem about the deeds of a great hero.

equinox In spring and in autumn, the point when day and night are of equal length.

excavate To dig in the ground to discover ancient remains.

exploits Brave deeds or adventures.

F

faience A type of opaque glass that is often blue or green. It is made from quartz or sand, lime, ash and natron.

figurine A small statue.

flax A blue-flowered plant grown for its fibre, which is used to make linen. It also has seeds that produce linseed oil.

foundation deposit A group of objects placed in the foundations of a temple by the king who built it.

furl To roll up the sail of a ship.

G

gazelle A small, graceful antelope.

genie A friendly spirit who drives away evil. Statues of genies appear on Mesopotamian palace walls blessing the king.

geometric pattern A pattern made by shapes such as lines, circles and triangles.

glazed bricks Baked bricks, with a colourful, glassy coating.

▼ *Ziggurat*

golden fly A badge given as a reward to soldiers in ancient Egypt for bravery in battle.

grid pattern A plan dividing towns into blocks and straight streets at right angles.

gypsum A type of limestone used for sculpture.

H

henna A reddish dye for the hair or skin, made from the leaves of a shrub.

hieratic A shorthand version of the Egyptian hieroglyphic script, used by priests.

hieroglyph A picture symbol used in ancient Egyptian writing.

high priest or priestess The chief priest or priestess in a temple, believed to have a special relationship with the deity.

hilt The handle of a sword or dagger.

I

impression The shape and pattern left on a clay tablet when a seal is pressed on to it.

incense Sweet-smelling gum or bark burnt as part of religious ceremonies.

indigo A dark blue dye taken from plants.

inscription Writing done with a reed pen on a clay tablet or with a chisel on stone.

▼ *Lamassus.*

irrigate To bring water to dry land, for example by pipes, canals or ditches.

ivory Elephant tusk, used to make items such as furniture, boxes and handles.

J

jackal A wild dog that lives in Asia and Africa.

K

knucklebones The small round bones in the feet of animals.

L

lamassu A huge stone statue of a human-headed bull or lion used to guard the entrance to a palace.

lapis lazuli A dark blue, semi-precious stone used for jewellery and seals.

libation A sacrifice of wine or oil poured out in honour of a god or goddess.

loom A frame on which cloth is woven.

Lower Egypt The northern part of Egypt, especially the Nile delta.

lute A stringed instrument like a small, round guitar.

lyre A stringed instrument similar to a harp.

▼ *Obelisk.*

M

Middle Kingdom
The period of Egyptian history between 2050 and 1786BC.

millennium A timespan of 1000 years.

mother-of-pearl The shiny material found inside shells, used to decorate furniture and musical instruments.

mummy The dead body of a human (or animal), preserved by drying.

mushushshu A dragon-like creature belonging to Marduk, god of Babylon.

myth A traditional story, often telling of gods, goddesses or strange creatures, which attempts to explain the creation of the world or how the natural world works.

N

natron Salty crystals, used in preparing mummies.

New Kingdom The period of Egyptian history between 1550–1070BC.

▲ *Gold coffin mask of Tutankhamun.*

▼ *Ancient city of Nimrud on the banks of the river Tigris.*

Nilometer A series of measured steps or a column used to measure the depth of the Nile floods.

nomadic Not leading a settled life, moving from one place to another

O

oasis A place in a desert area where there is water.

obelisk A tall, slender, tapering, needle-like column of stone, erected as a monument.

ochre A red or yellow earth.

Old Kingdom The period of Egyptian history between 2686 and 2181BC.

overlord The ruler of a large state who demands loyalty and tribute from a ruler of a smaller state or city.

P

papyrus A tall reedy plant that grows in the river Nile. It is used for making paper.

pendant A piece of jewellery hung on a chain around the neck.

pharaoh The ruler of ancient Egypt.

pigment A colouring used in paint.

potter's wheel A round slab, spun round to help shape the wet clay when making pots by hand.

prism In archaeology, a hollow, three-dimensional clay tablet with six or eight sides.

province Part of an empire ruled by a governor on behalf of a king.

prow The front end of a ship.

purification The means by which a king or priest made himself clean so as to be fit to offer sacrifices to his god.

pyramid A large pointed monument with a broad, square base and triangular sides.

Q

quarry A place where building stone can be dug out of the ground.

R

relief A carved stone slab in which images appear raised from the background.

ritual A religious ceremony.

S

saffron An orange powder taken from crocus flowers, used as a spice or a dye.

sanctuary The most holy place in a temple.

sarcophagus The stone casing for a coffin.

sceptre A rod carried by a king, queen or emperor as an emblem of rule.

scribe A professional writer, a clerk or civil servant.

script The type of symbols used in a method of writing.

sculpture Carved figures of stone, wood or metal.

▲ *Early Egyptian carving of a horse.*

Semitic A family of languages that includes Akkadian, Aramaic and modern Hebrew and Arabic.

serfs People who are not free to move from the land they farm without the permission of their lord.

shaduf A bucket on a weighted pole, used to move water from the river Nile into the fields on the banks.

shrine A container of holy relics, a place for worship.

side lock A plait of hair worn by children in ancient Egypt.

sistrum A metal rattle, used as a musical instrument.

solstice Midsummer or midwinter.

Sphinx A mythical creature with a woman's head and a lion's body.

spindle A rod used to twist fibres into yarn while spinning.

stela An upright slab or pillar bearing an inscription or carved image.

stern The rear end of a ship.

strike A work stoppage, part of a demand for better conditions.

superstition An illogical belief in good luck or bad luck.

survey To measure land or buildings.

T

tablet A flat piece of clay of varying shape and size used for cuneiform writing in Mesopotamia.

tax Goods, money or services paid to the government.

temple A special building where offerings are made to a god or goddess.

terracotta Brown-red earthenware pottery or sculpture, fired in a kiln.

textile Any cloth produced by the process of weaving.

treaty An agreement made between different cities, countries, kings or their vassals.

tribute Goods given by a country to its conquerors, as a mark of submission.

turquoise A blue-green semi-precious stone.

U
Underworld The 'land of the dead', where one goes after death.

Upper Egypt The southern part of Egypt.

V
vassal The ruler of a small state who acknowledges a greater king as his overlord. He promises to be loyal and pay tribute while his overlord promises to protect him.

vizier The treasurer or highest-ranking official in the Egyptian court.

W
weir A low dam built across a river or canal to control the flow of water.

winged disc A symbol of the sun god Shamash or of Ashur, the chief god of Assyria.

Z
ziggurat A solid, stepped pyramid built of mud-brick, with a small temple on top.

▲ *Assyrian royal chariot.*

Index

◀ Lamassus.

▲ *Painting of what the city of Ashur might have been like.*

▶ *Make a necklace, see pages 90–1.*

▲ *Great Sphinx.*

▲ *Make a lyre, see pages 86–7.*

▼ *Pyramid in Egypt.*